# The Case for Moderate Growth in Vehicle Miles of Travel: A Critical Juncture in U.S. Travel Behavior Trends

Prepared for

U.S. Department of Transportation
Office of the Secretary of Transportation
400 Seventh Street, S.W.
Washington, D.C. 20590

Steven E. Polzin, Ph.D.

Center for Urban Transportation Research
University of South Florida
4202 Fowler Ave. CUT100
Tampa, Florida 33620-5375

**April 2006**

CUTR

| 1. Report No. | 2. Government Accession No. | 3. Recipient's Catalog No. |
|---|---|---|
| **4. Title and Subtitle** The Case For Moderate Growth in Vehicle Miles of Travel: A Critical Juncture in U.S. Travel Behavior Trends | | **5. Report Date** April 2006 |
| | | **6. Performing Organization Code** |
| **7. Author(s)** Steven E. Polzin, PhD. | | **8. Performing Organization Report No.** |
| **9. Performing Organization Name and Address** Center for Urban Transportation Research, University of South Florida 4202 Fowler Avenue, CUT100 Tampa, FL 33620-5375 | | **10. Work Unit No. (TRAIS)** |
| | | **11. Contract or Grant No.** |
| **12. Sponsoring Agency Name and Address** U.S. Department of Transportation Office of the Secretary of Transportation 400 Seventh Street, S.W. Washington, D.C. 20590 | | **13. Type of Report and Period Covered** Final Report |
| | | **14. Sponsoring Agency Code** |

**15. Supplementary Notes**

Prepared in cooperation with the USDOT

**16. Abstract**

This report hypothesizes that the United States has reached a critical juncture in terms of national mobility trends and underlying socio-demographic conditions and travel behavior that will result in more moderate rates of annual vehicle miles of travel (VMT) growth in the future. However, slower VMT growth may not portend lower rates of congestion growth.

This report explores the major factors that influence travel behavior. The indirect factors are discussed first using primarily empirical data. These are divided into three major categories: socio-economic conditions, land use conditions, and transportation system conditions. This report concentrates most on the role of the socio-economic conditions and travel behavior followed by a discussion of the direct factors. Several of these factors appear to be undergoing historic trend reversals. In addition, new evidence suggests that congestion levels have reached the point where average travel speeds are declining. This declining speed may provide additional dampening of VMT growth.

Two forecasts of future VMT are produced that build on the data and information presented in the body of the report.

This report is intended to stimulate thinking about the future trends in travel demand and the underlying factors that influence those trends.

| **17. Key Word** vehicle miles of travel, travel demand, travel behavior, trip generation, trip length, mode choice, transit, National Household Travel Survey, National Personal Travel Survey | **18. Distribution Statement** **No Restriction** This report is available to the public through the NTIS, Springfield, VA 22161 | | |
|---|---|---|---|
| **19. Security Classif. (of this report)** Unclassified | **20. Security Classif. (of this page)** Unclassified | **21. No. of Pages** 48 | **22. Price** No cost |

Form DOT F 1700.7 (B-72)

## ACKNOWLEDGEMENT

The research that underlies this report has been supported by several different research initiatives sponsored by the Florida Department of Transportation and USDOT and carried out by CUTR.  This includes investigations of trends and conditions in transportation, investigation of VMT relationships with land use, and the travel behavior of the public as revealed by analysis of the National Household Travel Survey data.

Various CUTR researchers including Dr. Xuehao Chu, Dr. Edward Mierzejewski, Lavenia Toole-Holt, and Edward Maggio have participated in or provided input to the analyses.  The support and feedback of clients and colleagues is appreciated, as is USDOT's interest in supporting the publication and dissemination of this report.  It is hoped the report will be helpful in supporting informed transportation planning and policymaking.

## DISCLAIMER

## TABLE OF CONTENTS

Form DOT F 1700.7 (B-72)............................................................................................... ii

ACKNOWLEDGEMENT ..................................................................................................... iii

DISCLAIMER..................................................................................................................... iii

TABLE OF CONTENTS..................................................................................................... iv

LIST OF FIGURES ............................................................................................................. v

LIST OF TABLES .............................................................................................................. vi

EXECUTIVE SUMMARY.................................................................................................... vii

INTRODUCTION ................................................................................................................. 1
      Prior Forecasts of Slowing VMT Growth ................................................................ 3
      Conceptual Model of VMT Growth Drivers.............................................................. 4
      The Role of Freight and Long Distance Travel in VMT Growth ............................... 5

SOCIO-ECONOMIC CONDITIONS AND TRAVEL .............................................................. 7
      The Population Age Profile and VMT ...................................................................... 7
      Household Size and Structure ................................................................................ 8
      Labor Force Participation ....................................................................................... 9
      Auto and License Availability ................................................................................ 10
      The Role of Real Income Growth Driving VMT ..................................................... 12
      Vehicle Availability ............................................................................................... 15
      Time Use and Travel Time.................................................................................... 16

LAND USE INFLUENCES ON TRAVEL ............................................................................ 19

TRANSPORTATION SYSTEM INFLUENCE ON TRAVEL.................................................. 21

DIRECT DRIVERS OF TRAVEL BEHAVIOR .................................................................... 23
      *Population as a Contributor to VMT Growth* ......................................................... 23
      *Trip Rates as a Contributor to VMT Growth*......................................................... 23
      *Trip Length as a Contributor to VMT Growth* ....................................................... 23
      *Mode Shifts as a Contributor to VMT Growth* ...................................................... 24
            *Walking Mode Share* ..................................................................................... 24
            *Transit Mode Share* ....................................................................................... 25
            *Carpooling* ..................................................................................................... 26

VMT GROWTH................................................................................................................. 29
      VMT Growth by 2025 .......................................................................................... 30
      Forecast Results ................................................................................................. 32

POLICY IMPLICATIONS ................................................................................................... 33
      Congestion Implications of Future VMT Growth ................................................... 33

SUMMARY....................................................................................................................... 35

REFERENCES ................................................................................................................. 37

LIST OF FIGURES

Figure 1 – Population and VMT Changes ............................................................................... 1
Figure 2 – Annual Incremental Growth in VMT .................................................................... 2
Figure 3 – Annual Change in Population VMT ....................................................................... 3
Figure 4 – Conceptual Model of VMT Growth Drivers ......................................................... 4
Figure 5 – Truck Share of VMT .............................................................................................. 5
Figure 6 – U.S. Population Age Distribution with Annual VMT and PMT per Capita ................. 7
Figure 7 – Average Household Size ........................................................................................ 9
Figure 8 – Household Size Composition ................................................................................. 9
Figure 9 – Annual Trips and VMT by Household Size .......................................................... 9
Figure 10 – Labor Force Participation Trend by Gender ...................................................... 10
Figure 11 – Driving Population by Age and Gender ............................................................. 10
Figure 12 – Share of Population 16 and Older with Licenses .............................................. 11
Figure 13 – Vehicle Availability ............................................................................................ 11
Figure 14 – Share of Zero Vehicle Households .................................................................... 12
Figure 15 – Income Distribution by Auto Availability ........................................................... 12
Figure 16 – Household Income and Expenditure per VMT .................................................. 14
Figure 17 – Daily Person Trip Rate by Vehicle Availability ................................................. 15
Figure 18 – Reported Travel Time to Work .......................................................................... 16
Figure 19 – Change in Time Allocation Since 1965 ............................................................. 17
Figure 20 – Time Spent in Travel Daily ................................................................................ 17
Figure 21 – Average Annual Time Use Change from 1985 to 2001 .................................... 18
Figure 22 – Influence of Land Use on Travel ....................................................................... 20
Figure 23 – Share of Urban VMT by Road Type, 1966 - 2001 ........................................... 21
Figure 24 – Changes in Travel Speed Over Time ................................................................ 22
Figure 25 – Person Trips Per Trip Length ............................................................................ 23
Figure 26 – NPTS and NHTS Work Trip Walking Mode Shares .......................................... 24
Figure 27 – Census Work Trip Percent Walking to Work Mode Share ................................ 25
Figure 28 – Transit Mode Share Trends - Survey Data ....................................................... 25
Figure 29 – Urban Public Transportation Mode Share, Person Miles of Travel Based .......... 26
Figure 30 – Census Work Trip Carpooling Mode Share ...................................................... 26
Figure 31 – Vehicle Occupancies – NHTS/NPTS ................................................................ 27
Figure 32 – Vehicle Miles of Travel per Person Miles of Travel ......................................... 27
Figure 33 – VMT Growth Contributors ................................................................................. 28
Figure 34 – Share of VMT Growth Attributable to Component Factors 1977-2001 ............. 28
Figure 35 – VMT per Person Hour Spent Traveling ............................................................ 31
Figure 36 – VMT Growth Scenario, Formula 1 .................................................................... 32
Figure 37 – VMT Growth Scenario, Formula 2 .................................................................... 32
Figure 38 – Standard Roadway Speed-Volume Relationship .............................................. 34

LIST OF TABLES

Table 1 – Household VMT, Income, and Transportation Spending ............................................. 13
Table 2 – Summary NPTS and NHTS Data and Key Indicators ................................................. 29

## EXECUTIVE SUMMARY

There is substantial evidence that the United States has reached a critical juncture in national mobility trends and underlying socio-demographic conditions and travel behavior. This report provides insight into future demand for travel by reviewing the underlying trends and producing two scenario forecasts of travel demand. As transportation professionals seek to address future transportation needs, a rich understanding of underlying factors contributes to the ability to forecast and plan for future needs. This analysis suggests that changes in trends are likely to result in more moderate rates of annual vehicle miles of travel (VMT) growth in the future. However, the non-linear relationship between VMT and congestion is such that slower VMT growth may not portend lower rates of congestion growth.

This report explores trends for several of the major factors that influence travel behavior. The underlying factors are discussed first using empirical trend data. These are divided into three major categories: socio-economic conditions, land use conditions, and transportation system conditions. This report concentrates most on the role of the socio-economic conditions and travel behavior. Factors considered include population age profile, auto availability, licensure rates, household size, shared ride propensity, transit use propensity, walk propensity, male and female labor force participation, real income per capita, and land use patterns. Several of these factors appear to be undergoing historic trend stabilization or reversals for their respective metrics. These include:

- Stabilizing average household size following decades of declines,
- Stabilizing female labor force participation rates following decades of increases,
- Stabilizing female share of licensed drivers following decades of increases,
- Stabilizing share of zero-vehicle households following decades of decreases,
- Transition of the baby boom population bubble through their peak travel years.

The relationship between transportation system performance and travel is discussed and evidence is presented that itemizes trend changes. The trends include:

- Stabilizing or declining average travel speed following years of increases,
- A change from declining to modest increases in vehicle travel cost,
- Stabilizing public transit mode shares following decades of declines,
- Stabilizing auto occupancies following decades of declines,
- Stabilizing mode share for walk and bike travel following decades of declines.

Trends whose future direction is less clear include:

- The modest trip length growth trend appears to be continuing
- The rapid growth in trip frequency appears to be slowing
- The rapid increase in per capita time spent on travel appears to be continuing.

Using this context as a background, future VMT growth scenarios were developed that extrapolate from the data and information presented in the body of the report. Two different derivations for calculating total person VMT were developed. Historical changes in each formula factor were determined and based on historical changes in each component; two scenarios of future VMT growth were developed.

Formula 1:   $$\text{Population} \times \frac{\text{Person Trips}}{\text{Person}} \times \frac{\text{Person Miles}}{\text{Person Trip}} \times \frac{\text{Vehicle Miles}}{\text{Person Mile}} = \text{Vehicle Miles of Travel}$$

Formula 2:   $$\text{Population} \times \frac{\text{Person Hours}}{\text{Person}} \times \frac{\text{Vehicle Miles}}{\text{Person Hour}} = \text{Vehicle Miles of Travel}$$

Historical trend data from 1977- 2001, were reviewed and a scenario forecast for 2025 was developed. Formula 1 was applied with the Census estimate of 22 percent population growth, an assumed 16 percent increase in person trips per person (trip rate), an 8 percent increase in person miles per person trip (trip length), and a 5 percent increase in vehicle miles of travel per person mile (measure of mode share). This set of assumptions produced a total growth in VMT of 60 percent.

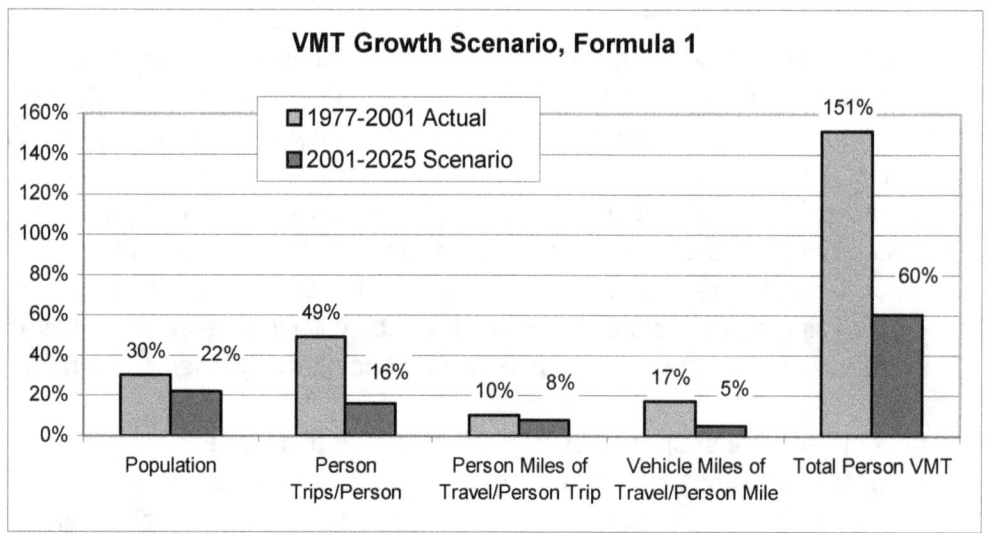

Formula 2 was applied with the same population increase estimate, an assumed 35 percent increase in travel time budgets, and an assumed 8 percent decline in VMT per person hour of travel (a composite measure of travel speed and mode share). This produced an estimate of increased VMT of 51 percent. The 60 percent increase is approximately 2 percent per year. The 51 percent increase is the equivalent of 1.74 percent per year, slightly more modest. Both scenarios are well below historical averages but above the levels in three of the last four years, and significant in absolute terms and in terms of the need to expand capacity to accommodate demand.

The summary table details the changes in these factors and the numbers used in the development of the two scenarios.

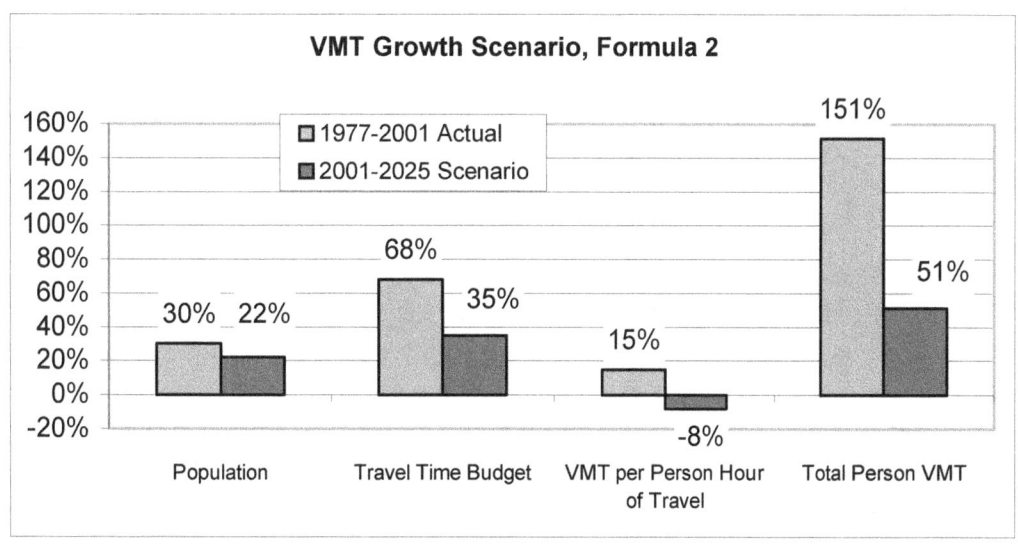

**VMT Growth Scenario, Formula 2**

**Summary of VMT Trends and Scenarios**

| Formula 1 | 1977-2001 Actual | 2001-2025 Scenario 1 |
|---|---|---|
| Population | 30.1% | 21.9% |
| Person Trips/Person | 49.2% | 16.0% |
| Person Miles of Travel/Person Trip | 10.4% | 8.0% |
| Vehicle Miles of Travel/Person Mile | 17.4% | 5.0% |
| Total Person VMT Change, 24 Years | 151.4% | 60.3% |

| Formula 2 | 1977-2001 Actual | 2001-2025 Scenario 2 |
|---|---|---|
| Population | 30.1% | 21.9% |
| Travel Time Budget | 68.2% | 35.0% |
| VMT per Person Hour of Travel | 14.9% | -8.0% |
| Total Person VMT Change, 24 Years | 151.4% | 51.4% |

While this report builds an empirical and theoretical case for slowing VMT growth nationally, it hypothesizes that there may continue to be declining system performance (speed) in spite of slower VMT growth due to the fact that more of the roadway system is at or near critical congestion levels and, hence, more susceptible to performance deterioration with modest increases in travel demand. The report also suggests that the land use pattern impacts on travel behavior and person travel time budget growth are not well understood and a possible weak link in reaching conclusions about the ultimate course of VMT growth.

Collectively, this body of data provides a compelling case for moderating VMT growth. However, unanticipated phenomena such as the apparent unrelenting growth in travel time budgets and growing trip lengths may offset some of the factors that would appear to dampen VMT growth pressures. Similarly, fuel shortages or ongoing rapid price increases could dampen travel demand below the scenario levels. The report also suggests that transportation planners are not particularly expert at predicting how the overall roadway system will perform and how travelers may adapt their travel behaviors when faced with future levels of travel demand. The premise that the reserve capacity in our system has been nearly fully absorbed and travelers have made the easy adjustments in travel departure times and route choices to utilize the high performing roadway segments suggests that subsequent increases in demand may result in proportionately more severe consequences in terms of congestion levels and declining speeds.

This report identifies a host of potentially significant unknowns that ultimately will influence future travel. Many of these, such as the socio-demographic and economic trends, have been long acknowledged as issues that will influence the future demands on and performance of our transportation system. These include such topics as the impact of higher fuel costs, the impacts of older Americans driving more than in prior generations, and the ongoing consequences of changing household composition. Other unknowns suggest potentially new research needs and topics for policy analysis. These include developing a richer understanding of how the overall transportation system will perform when subject to greater demands, exploring causal factors and constraints to the growth in travel time expenditures by Americans, and understanding how evolving land use trends will impact both the need and the desire to travel.

While there is evidence to suggest more modest VMT growth in the future, there will continue to be huge transportation challenges and opportunities as professionals strive to understand, forecast, plan for, and deliver transportation infrastructure and services to meet the traveling public's needs. The set of factors that have most significantly influenced travel behavior and demand in the past may be changing, and our ability to understand which factors are critical in driving future travel demand will impact our ability to predict and respond to traveler needs. Understanding and preparing for long-range travel demands will remain critically important.

## INTRODUCTION

There is evidence that the United States has reached a critical juncture in terms of national mobility trends and socio-demographic conditions that will result in more moderate rates of annual vehicle miles of travel (VMT) growth in the future. However, slower VMT growth may not portend lower rates of congestion growth. Trends in VMT in recent years confirm moderating VMT growth, and numerous supporting trends provide a logical basis for presuming that lower VMT growth rates will be sustained going forward, absent a radical shift in demographic or economic conditions. As portrayed in Figure 1, since 1977, total person VMT for daily travel has grown by 151 percent, according to National Household Travel survey series data (NHTS/NPTS), and overall VMT has grown by over 90 percent, according to federal VMT databases[1]. This compares to population growth of approximately 30 percent. Thus, less than 30 percent of personal VMT growth is attributable to population growth. The remaining growth is attributable to a host of other factors that each contributes to VMT rates per capita or per household. These factors include population age profile, auto availability, licensure rates, household size, shared ride propensity, transit use propensity, walk propensity, male and female labor force participation, real income per capita, and land use patterns. In addition, new evidence suggests that congestion levels have reached the point where average travel speeds are declining. This declining speed may provide additional dampening of VMT growth if travelers are unwilling to increase the amount of time they spend on travel.

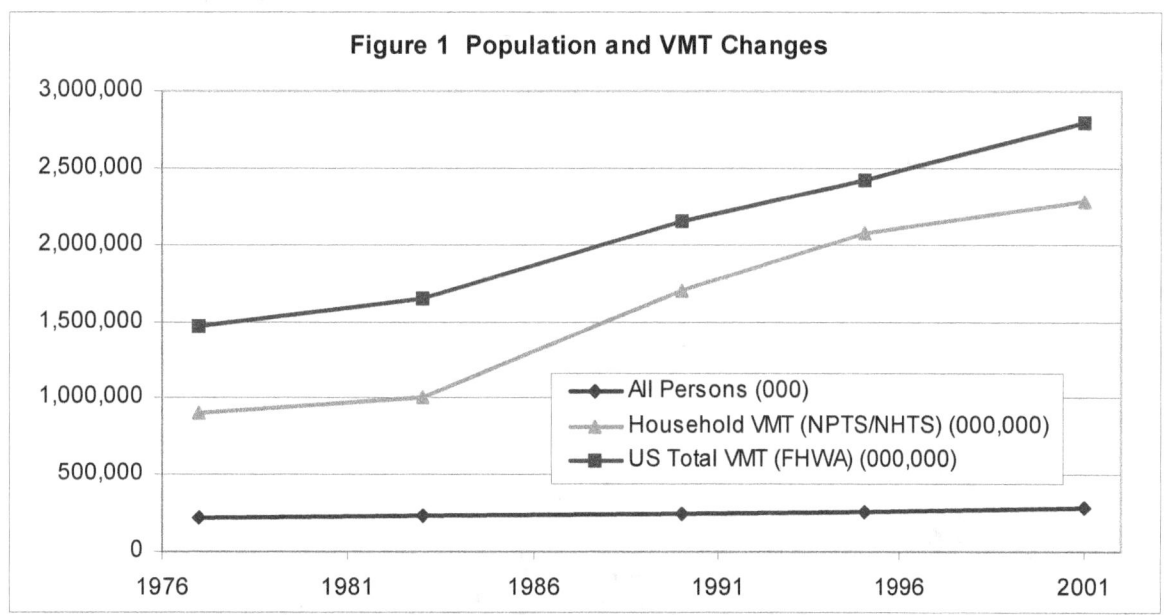

Source: VMT from Table VM-1, FHWA Highway Statistics Series, http://www.fhwa.dot.gov/policy/ohpi/hss/hsspubs.htm. NHTS/NPTS data from *Summary of Travel Trends 2001 National Household Travel Survey*, December 2004, Table 1, Page 9.

---

[1] Differences between NHTS and FHWA VMT growth percentages are due to a number of factors including the different base for calculating percent changes, survey affects for NHTS/NPTS data, and the inclusion of all traffic in the FHWA measure. Both sources showed a similar increment of growth over the 1977 to 2001 time period.

While this report builds a case for moderating VMT growth, it hypothesizes that there may continue to be declining travel speed in spite of slower VMT growth due to the fact that more of the roadway system is at or beyond capacity and, hence, more susceptible to deteriorating performance with modest increases in travel demand. It also suggests that the impacts of land use patterns on travel behavior and person travel time budget growth are not fully understood and possibly weak links in reaching conclusions about the ultimate course of VMT growth.

A formula for estimating VMT is developed and two scenarios of future VMT are produced that build on the data and information presented in the body of the report. While this report analyzes national trends, many of the observations are relevant across the country and, where data are available, the reader can compare local conditions against national norms to reflect on the relevance of the findings on a particular state or area.

Figure 2 shows annual VMT growth increments. These annual increments of VMT growth for all counted roadway travel (daily local person, long-distance person, and freight) have not grown since 1988 in spite of an ever larger population base. The figure also shows the uneven nature of VMT growth rates over time. Figure 3 presents annual and five-year rolling average VMT growth rates for total vehicle travel. As these graphs reveal, VMT growth has slowed to where the annual growth rates are below two percent. It is admittedly difficult to discern short-term effects such as the impact of the slower economy in the early 2000's, the trend for larger shares of intercity travel via auto as opposed to air since September 11, 2001, and the impact of energy prices in more recent years, from longer-term underlying trends. The 2005 increment in VMT growth (preliminary) was the lowest since 1980 and per capita VMT actually declined. Figure 3 also shows the population growth rate which can be compared to VMT five-year average growth rates. VMT growth remained over twice the rate of population until 2005 when population growth exceeded VMT growth.

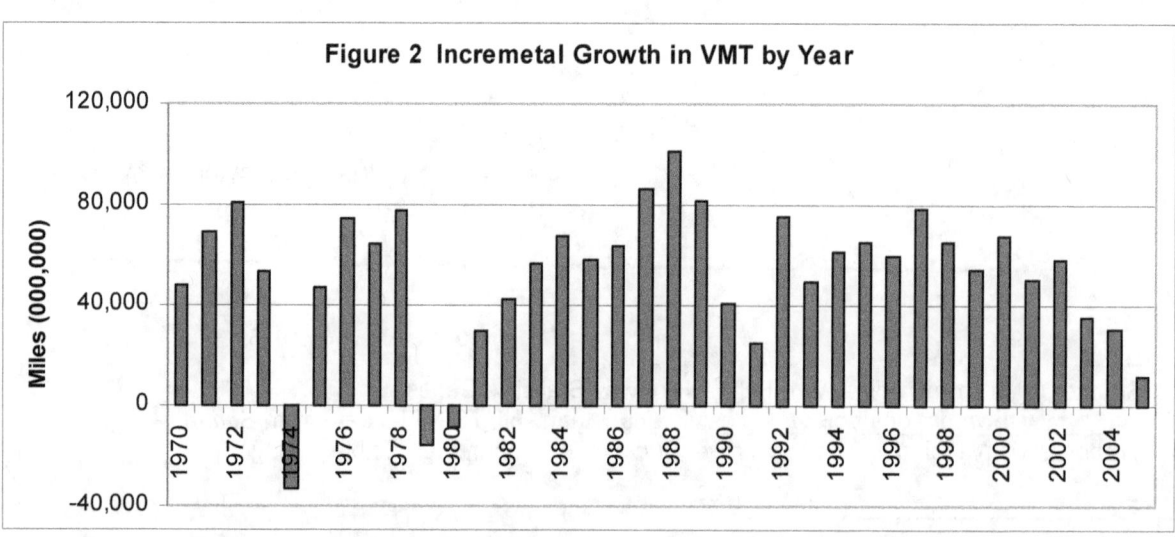

Source: CUTR analysis of FHWA VMT data.

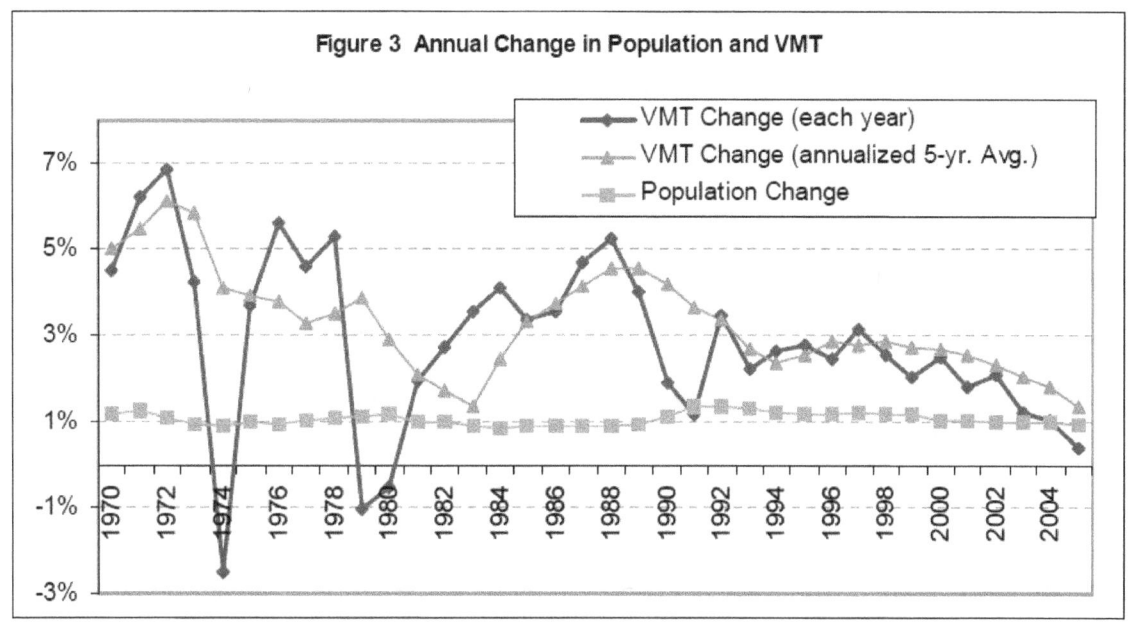

Figure 3 Annual Change in Population and VMT

Source: CUTR Analysis of FHWA VMT data.

## Prior Forecasts of Slowing VMT Growth

There were forecasts of slowing VMT growth more than a decade ago. Among the most comprehensive was an unpublished working paper by Charles Lave that spoke to the saturation effects of auto availability and the changing demographics as factors that would dampen the growth in VMT. Factors included were changes in labor force participation, age, income, and vehicle availability. The provocative title, "Things Won't Get a Lot Worse: The Future of U.S. Traffic Congestion," acknowledged the expectation that perhaps extrapolation of VMT trends were inappropriate, given the changes taking place in the economy and society (Lave 1991). This report revisits those and other trends to reassess current conditions.

More recent investigations of VMT growth include a variety of documents such as, "Aggregate Vehicle Mile Forecasting Model," (U.S. Department of Energy, 1995), which reviews VMT forecasting issues including sensitivities to age, income, and licensure rates. Oak Ridge National Laboratory has operated a similar aggregate travel forecasting model (Greene et al. 1995). An international forecast of travel demand that focuses on the relationship between person travel and economic development also is widely cited (Schafer and Victor 1997). "Factors That Affect VMT Growth" provides a comprehensive review of factors contributing to VMT growth (Schaper and Patterson 1998). This document investigates future VMT as a component in understanding future energy use and forecasts of VMT growth in the 1.5 to 2 percent per year range. The Transportation Sector Model of the National Energy Modeling System uses age and gender variables in its modeling of future VMT (U.S. Department of Energy 2001). Interestingly, much of the work providing long-range forecasts of travel demand have been motivated by energy use considerations rather than transportation infrastructure and service needs.

## Conceptual Model of VMT Growth Drivers

Travel or mobility is acknowledged to be a fundamentally important element in peoples' quality of life. Thus, travel is integral to peoples' activity patterns and is accordingly complex and influenced by a host of socio-economic characteristics of the traveler as well as by characteristics of the transportation system and other factors relating to culture, economic conditions, land use and public policy. The long history of studies of transportation has yielded a relatively uncontroversial sense of which factors are important considerations in travel behavior decisions. This conceptualization of travel behavior is the foundation for the four-step travel modeling framework that remains the principal basis for most travel forecasting (Martin 1998). Figure 4 outlines the major factors that influence travel behavior. The context factors are broader societal conditions that influence travel. The indirect factors are more specific conditions which are known to influence travel. Many of them are discussed in the report using empirical data. They are divided into three major categories: 1) socio-economic conditions, 2) land use conditions, and, 3) transportation system conditions. That is followed by a discussion of the direct factors that drive travel demand.

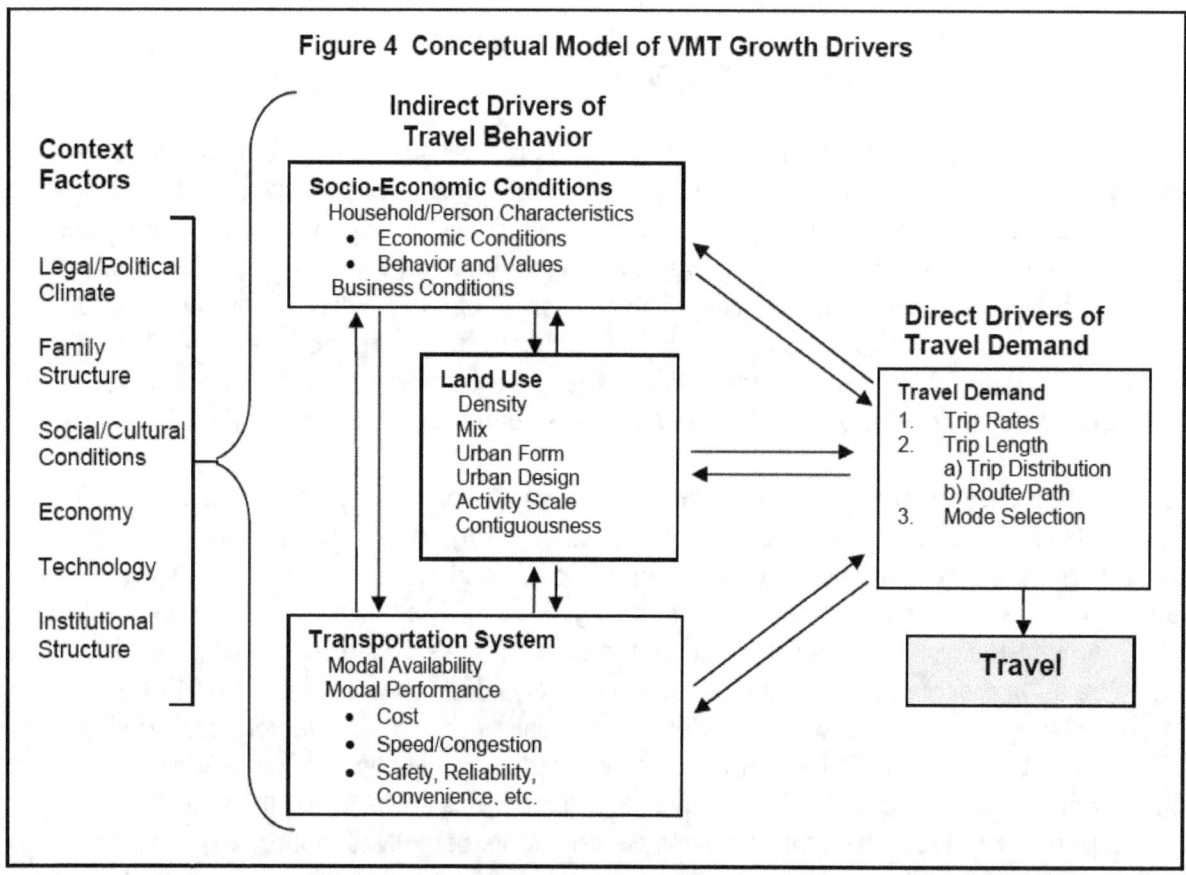

Source: CUTR Conceptualization of VMT Growth Drivers.

While this report discusses both the indirect and the direct drivers of travel it concentrates most specifically on the role of the socio-economic conditions and the transportation system characteristics on the growth of VMT. The interrelationships between the factors are strong, making it difficult to define precisely their relative importance. Yet, available data sheds substantial light on the significance of the various factors. Socio-economic conditions generate the demand for activities and the ability to afford travel. Land use patterns and the performance of the transportation system impact how that demand translates into specific demand for travel to various locations at various times via specific modes.

### The Role of Freight and Long Distance Travel in VMT Growth

Total VMT is the sum of three components: 1) person travel - the primary focus of this report, 2) commercial freight travel on the roadway system, and, 3) long distance intercity tourist and business travel by persons. Freight traffic growth has been an important factor in the growth of VMT, as truck traffic has increased faster than person travel. Its importance is accentuated because trucks have a disproportionate impact on roadway capacity. Depending on the context, a large truck can consume the equivalent of several cars worth of roadway capacity due to its physical size and its acceleration/braking and other performance characteristics.

Figure 5 shows the share of total VMT that is attributable to trucks (where trucks are defined as two-axle six-tire or larger vehicles). This more rapid growth in truck volume can be attributed to a number of factors including the dispersion of population and employment, the shift of significant freight activity from rail and other modes to truck, and the changes in the economy and business practices such as just-in-time deliveries of inventory items that increase delivery frequencies. Continuing dispersion of population and employment, growing real incomes driving demand for consumables, the globalization of the economy resulting in longer factory-

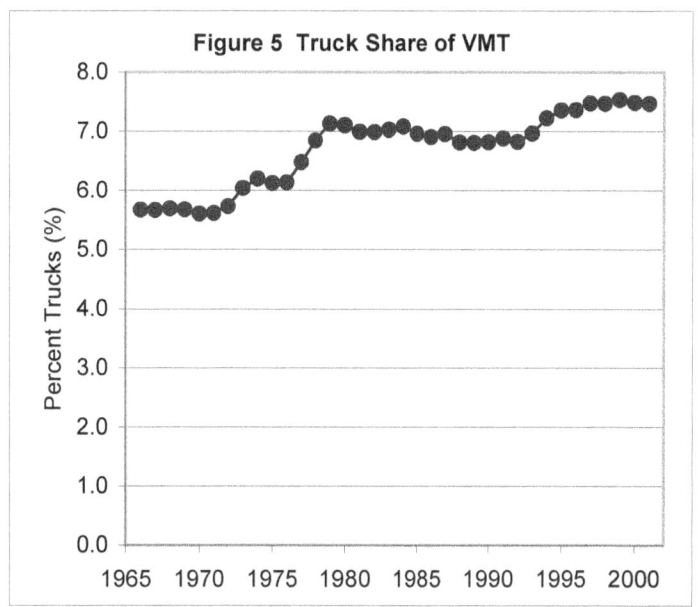

Source: US Department of Transportation, FHWA Highway Statistics Series.

to-consumer shipping distances, and continuing shifts to more frequent deliveries are expected to contribute to continued growth in truck VMT (Sedor and Caldwell 2002). While this research has not attempted to discern whether the historic trend of faster growth in truck VMT will continue or if some of the causal trends are fully played out, it is clear that many analysts anticipate continuing strong growth in truck VMT.

Long distance intercity travel by tourists and business travelers is an area where additional insight into recent and future trends would help enhance the overall understanding of VMT growth trends. While some long distance travel is not on the critical urban elements of the roadway system, the growing expanse of urban areas results in intercity travel demand increasingly interacting with local demand increasing overall congestion levels. Hence intercity travel is of interest to both state and urban area transportation planning.

## SOCIO-ECONOMIC CONDITIONS AND TRAVEL

Socio-economic conditions are known factors influencing travel behavior and among the variables used by transportation planners and modelers to understand and predict travel. Several characteristics of the population known to influence travel are discussed below.

### The Population Age Profile and VMT

Person travel is closely related to person activity levels, which are closely related to the lifecycle of the individual. Young children individually do not produce VMT but they create travel demands for parents. VMT levels grow with age and are at their highest level for young to middle-age adults who are in peak levels of both work-related travel as well as peak levels of household-serving travel. This is the stage where parents serve as chauffeurs to youth activities, travel to meet work and personal needs, and make other household-serving trips such as shopping and errands. Older adults historically have shown declines in travel, particularly when they are no longer burdened with work related and child-serving travel. As age increases, health and stamina levels typically dampen activity and travel levels. With age comes a shift away from accumulating material items toward consuming services. Income may also become a constraint on travel.

Figure 6 shows the person travel levels as a function of age in the vertical bars, one for person miles traveled (PMT) and one for VMT. Persons 35 to 50 year old are at their peak travel age.

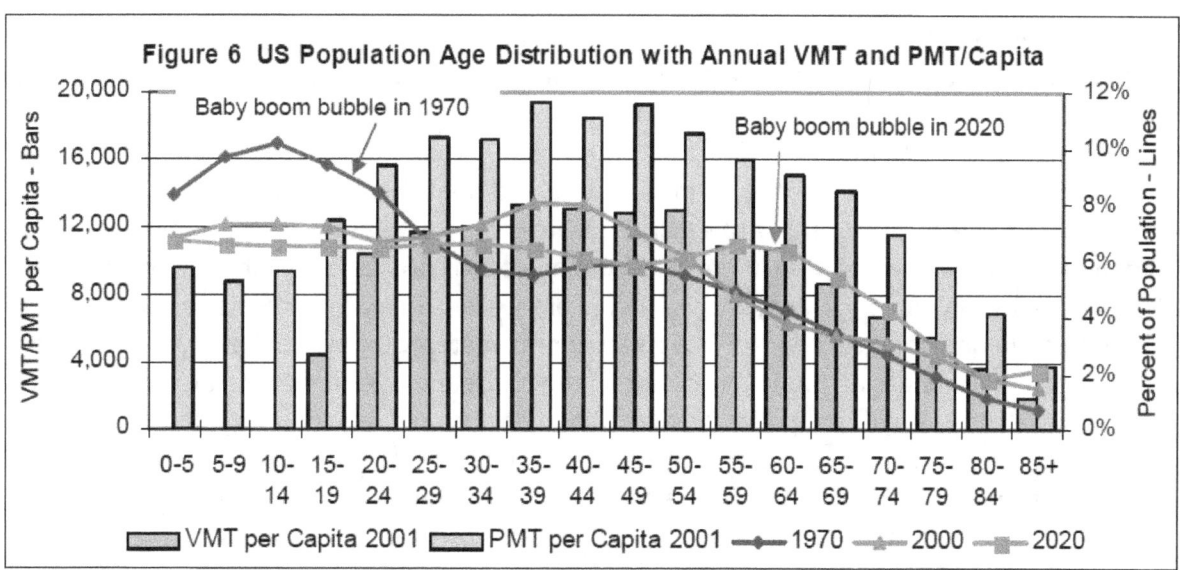

Source: CUTR analysis of NHTS/NPTS and Census data.

Figure 6 also shows the 1970, 2000, and 2020 age distributions of the population. As this figure reveals, the baby boom population bubble is currently situated in the peak travel years. Thus, the aging of the baby boom cohorts has been a contributor to travel demand growth as this large cohort has moved into peak travel ages. As this population segment continues to age, it will have a potential moderating impact on future travel demand growth as travel decreases with age.

In addition to the age distribution affect, PMT per capita has increased over time for all age cohorts. This is attributed to increasing vehicle travel requirements for youth due to dispersed suburban environments and working parents where ever greater shares of social activity are dependent on auto travel. For the older age groups, improved health, wealth, and higher licensure rates for older women have resulted in slower rates of declining mobility for older population segments. Middle aged population travel demand growth is attributed to active work participation, household member-serving activities and more out-of-home activities. The most recent 2001 NHTS data showed increased travel for all age groups including persons in the peak travel years.

While VMT rates may change over time, it is apparent that the age cohorts that are currently at their peak travel rates are the largest age cohorts in the population. The aging baby boomers are passing through their peak travel years. If it were assumed that VMT per capita for a given age cohort were stable over time, the age profile affect alone explains a few percent of the growth in VMT since 1970. Looking ahead, forecasted age profiles would be expected to result in a modest decline in VMT if VMT rates per person by age remain at current levels. While the age profile affect is modest in the context of the overall growth in travel demand, it is, nonetheless, shifting from a factor accelerating travel growth to one dampening demand.

Continued changes in vehicle travel rates by age can be expected. One of the population segments that has had rapid growth in VMT is young drivers as auto availability has increased. However, overall auto availability levels appear to be moderating as well. Another segment that has shown increasing mobility is the older adult population. As noted, improved health and income levels and growing auto availability and licensure rates, particularly among women, are responsible for more travel for these cohorts. Dispersed population (suburban living), smaller household size due to lower fertility rates, high divorce rates and lessened multi-generational living in the same household, and improved economic conditions also contribute to higher older adult VMT rates. In earlier generations, women were far less likely than men to have ever learned to drive and hold a license. For women approximately 50 years old and younger, this phenomenon is no longer as pronounced, and in the future the licensure rates are anticipated to remain high across all age groups for females and males. Improving longevity and health combined with additional technology aids to assist driving are likely to produce continuing growth in the elderly VMT. The following sections quantify some of these trends.

### Household Size and Structure

The makeup of American households has changed dramatically since the early part of the century. According to the U.S. Census Bureau, contributing factors include increased mobility, more affordable housing, women having fewer children, and an increase in diversity of the U.S. population. As Figure 7 shows, the average household size has been decreasing.

Since 1900, average household size has decreased by two persons per household. However, the rate of change in household size is slowing and the change from 1990 to 2000 is the lowest 10-year change of the century. Figure 8 shows the distribution of households by size. Between 1990 and 2000, for example, more rapid growth in one and two member households resulted in the share of households in these groups growing. As indicated in Figure 9, larger households appear to offer some economy of person travel as household-serving trips may be centralized and there are greater opportunities to carpooling which accommodates additional person trips without adding new vehicle trips. However, one should also note that two person households more than double the VMT of single person households. This may be a result of the fact that many single person households are elderly persons living alone who are not very mobile and other individuals who have chosen a more solitary lifestyle.

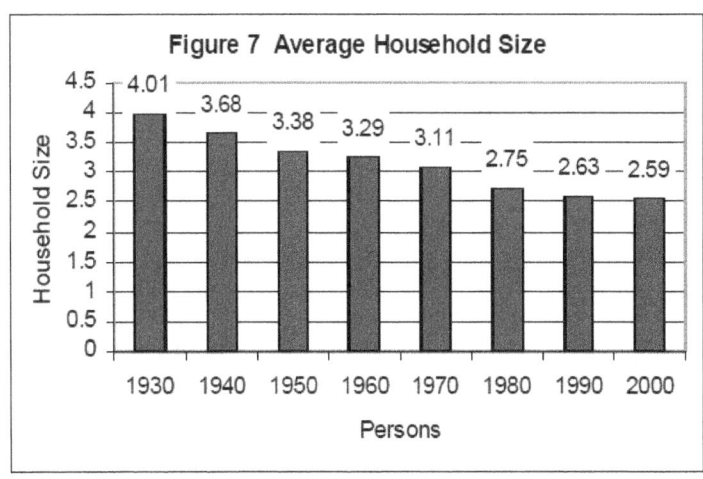

Source: Census data.

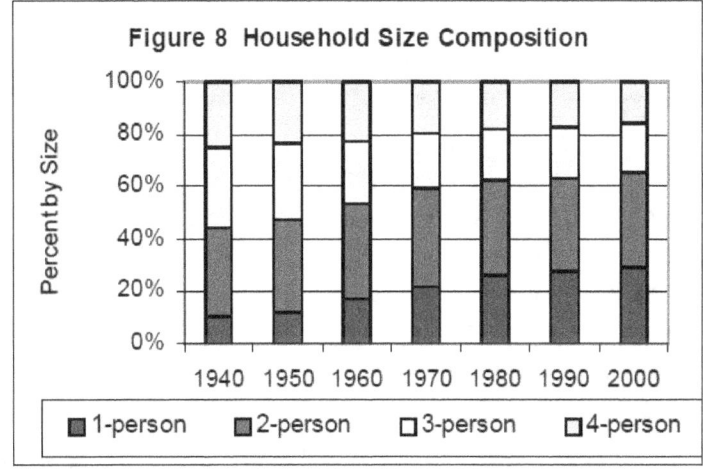

Source: Census Data.

**Labor Force Participation**

The labor force participation rates for men and women are displayed in Figure 10. The participation rate for women has increased since World War II, while the rate for males has decreased. Over the past decade, rates for both men and women have remained relatively constant, which may suggest that the labor force participation rates have reached equilibrium. Historically, analysts

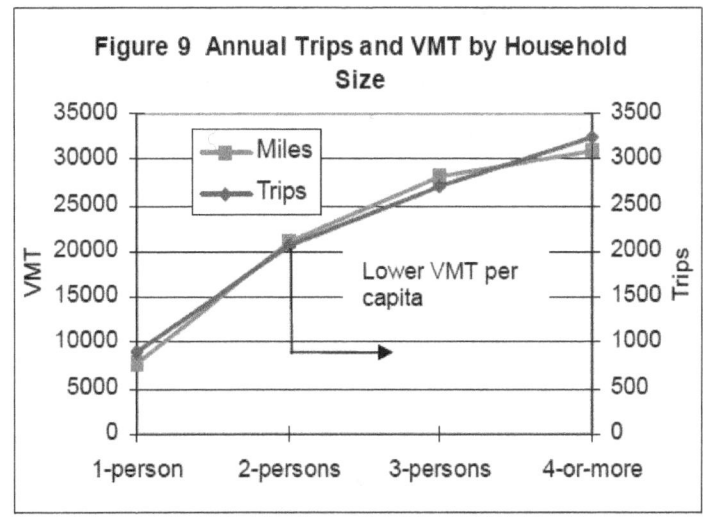

Source: CUTR analysis of NHTS data.

have assumed a lowering of the labor force participation rate as the baby boom generation reaches retirement. However, economic conditions and shifts in the nature of retirement may influence the age at which individuals leave the work force.

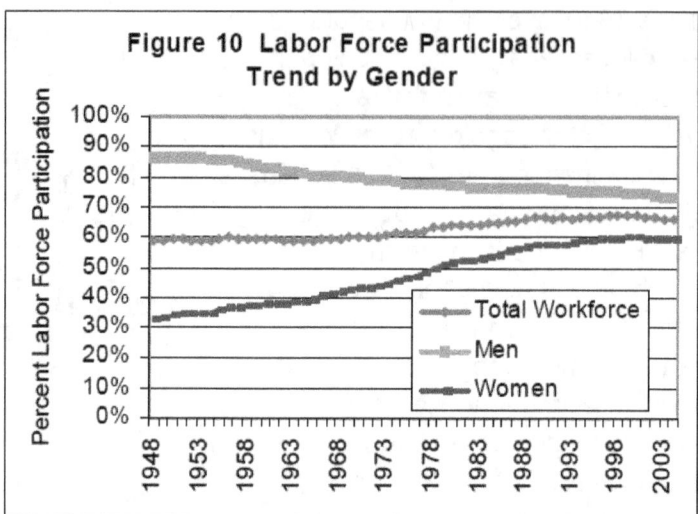

Source: US Department of Labor, Bureau of Labor Statistics, Employment Status of Civilian Population.

## Auto and License Availability

The availability of vehicles and driver's licenses in society contributes greatly to the mobility rates of the population and consequently to VMT levels. Over the past several decades, licensed drivers and personal vehicles have become increasingly abundant. In the past, it was less common for women to have a driver's license. However, in today's society, women hold half of all licenses in America. Figure 11 shows the share of licensed drivers by gender and age in 2000. The percent of drivers is the same for both sexes until about the age of 50, when the share of women drivers

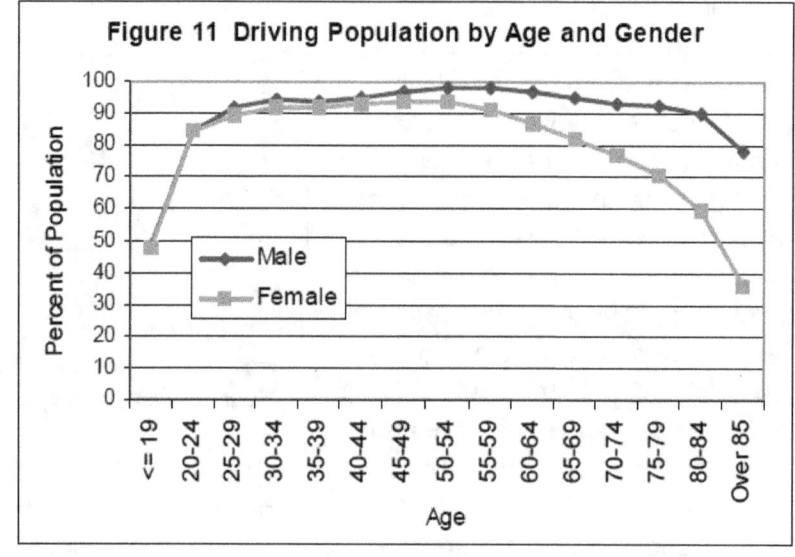

Source: FHWA, Highway Statistics Series, 2000.

begins to decrease. As the population ages, it is likely that the share of women drivers per age group will become more similar to men for all age groups as the younger female population will be accustomed to driving and having licenses.

Figure 12 shows the trend in increased license possession for women. The availability of vehicles has also increased over time. Figure 13 shows the trend in the ratio of vehicles to adults, drivers and workers. In 2001, the ratio of vehicles to workers and to drivers was over one while the ratio to adults approached one. This would indicate that each adult, driver, and worker has at least one vehicle available to him or her. Of course, the distribution of vehicles across the population is not even, with some households having no vehicle (also see Figure 17).

Figure 14 shows the trend in zero-car household shares. Some share of these are zero-car households by choice or due to medical/physical or legal reasons and not financial reasons. While the share of zero-car households has declined, the number of such households has only declined modestly from 11.4 million in 1969 to 10.9 in 2001. The number of persons in zero-car households has declined more significantly as average household size has declined.

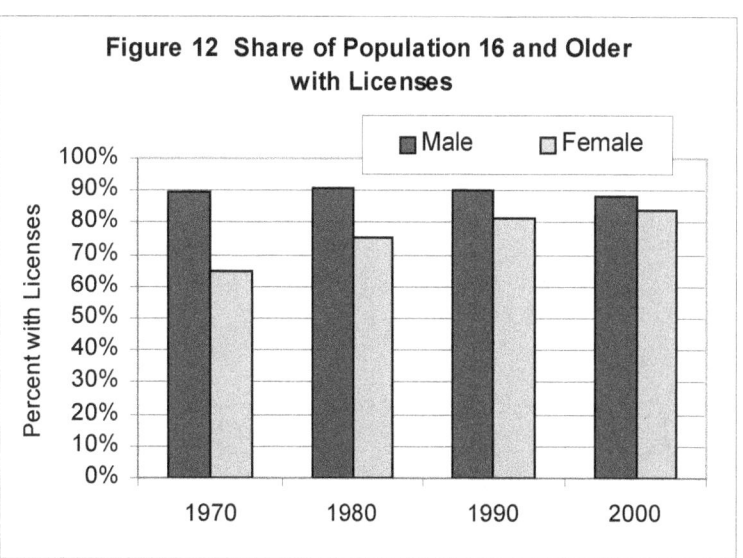

Source: U.S. Department of Transportation and U.S. Census.

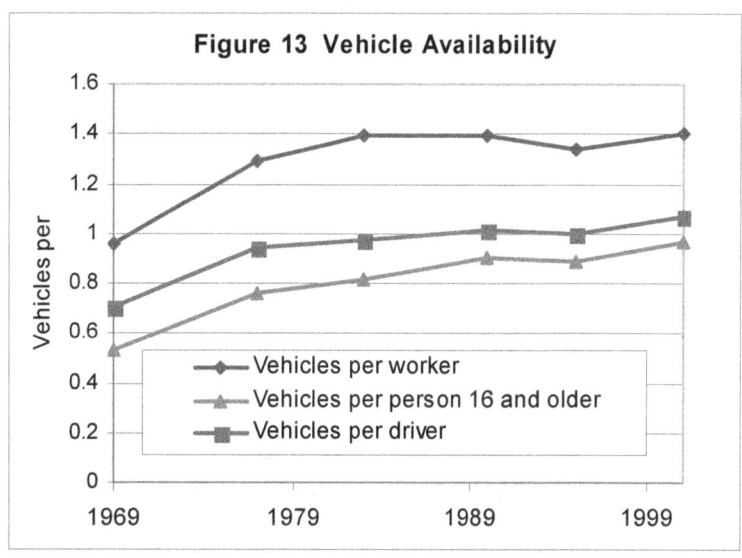

Source: CUTR analysis of NHTS/NPTS data.

Figure 15 shows the income distribution and vehicle availability of households. While overall economic growth may provide some additional shrinkage in the zero-car population segment, it is human nature that there will always be some share of the population with limited means, and others who will have legal, mental, emotional, or physical constraints that will keep them from becoming auto owners and operators. The size of the market of persons who choose not to own vehicles but who are otherwise able to is not known. There is speculation that a growing interest in central business district residential locations may increase the share of the population that chooses to not own a vehicle or as many vehicles.

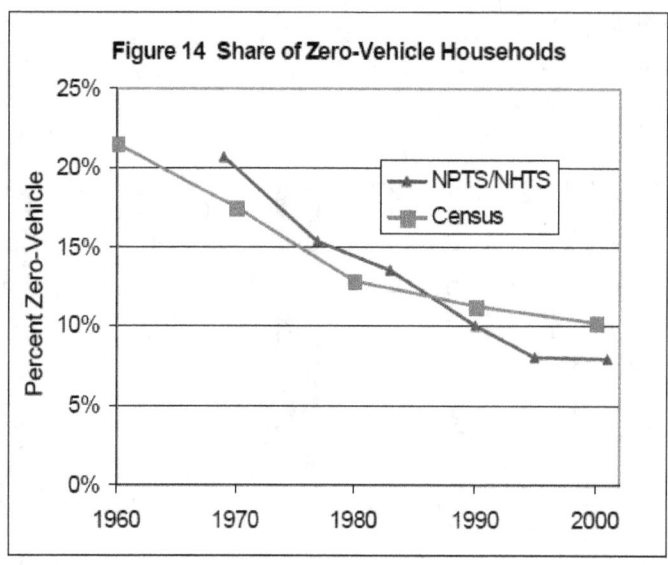

Source: CUTR analysis of NHTS/NPTS data.

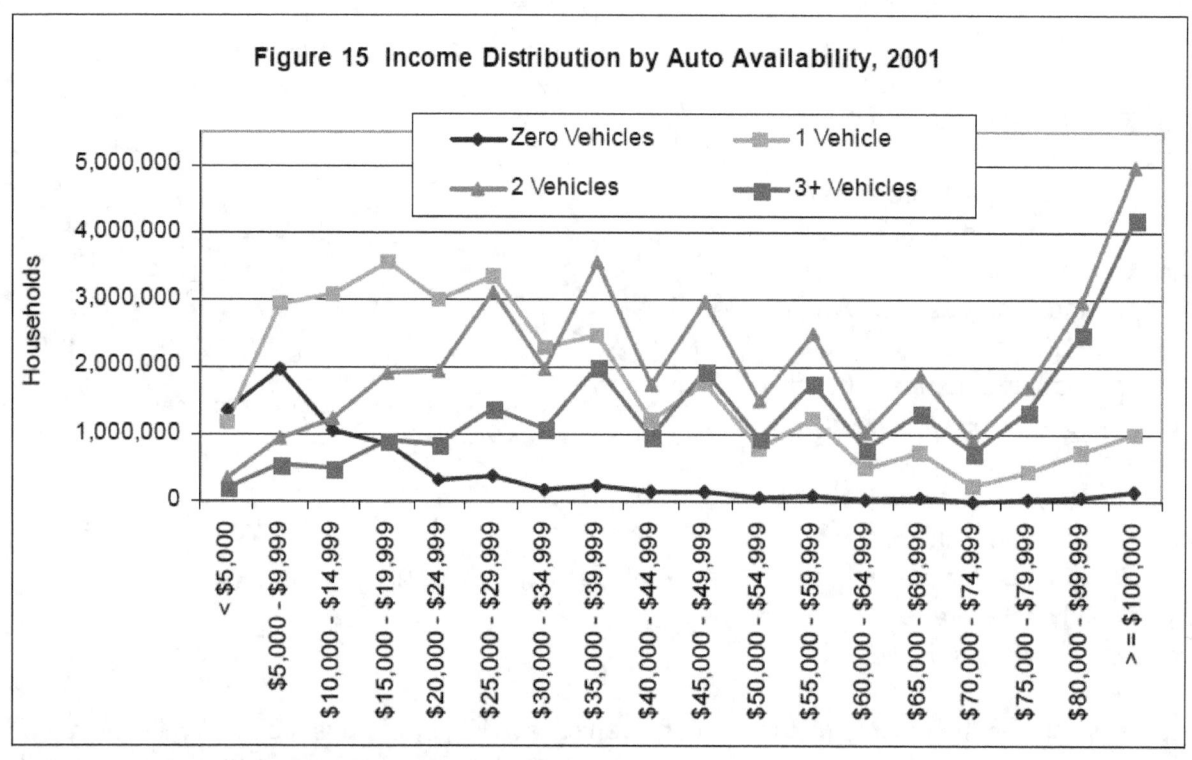

Source: CUTR analysis of 2001 NHTS data.

### The Role of Real Income Growth Driving VMT

Real income growth is considered one of the key factors in driving travel demand. The growth in real income drives travel demand by both enabling persons to afford to travel and creating a greater demand to participate in activities such as entertainment and shopping that are facilitated by higher real incomes. In addition to income, the real cost of travel influences travel demand. Real incomes and travel costs together determine the affordability of auto-based mobility.

Incomes are highly correlated with other factors such as population age profile, female labor force participation, and vehicle availability. Thus, causality of VMT growth needs to be evaluated in the context of this correlation between variables. One interesting observation from Table 1 is that household spending for travel has remained relatively constant over time with

#### Table 1 Household VMT, Income, and Transportation Spending

| Year | Consumer Price Index (1) | Household VMT (000,000) (2) | House-holds (000) | Persons (000) | Average Household Income after Taxes in Current Dollars (3) | Average Household Spending on POV in Current Dollars (3) | Average Household Income after Taxes in Constant 2001 Dollars (3) | Average Household Spending on POV in Constant 2001 Dollars (3) | POV Spending per VMT (cost per mile) in Constant Dollars | Income per Person in Constant Dollars |
|---|---|---|---|---|---|---|---|---|---|---|
| 1984 | 103.9 | 1,051,869 | 89,607 | 240,839 | $21,237 | $4,049 | $36,199 | $6,902 | $0.59 | $13,468 |
| 1990 | 130.7 | 1,695,290 | 93,347 | 239,416 | $28,937 | $4,818 | $39,210 | $6,528 | $0.36 | $15,288 |
| 1995 | 152.4 | 2,068,368 | 98,990 | 259,994 | $33,864 | $5,659 | $39,352 | $6,576 | $0.31 | $14,983 |
| 2001 | 177.1 | 2,281,863 | 107,369 | 277,208 | $44,587 | $7,233 | $44,587 | $7,233 | $0.34 | $17,270 |

Sources:  1. ftp://ftp.bls.gov/pub/special.requests/cpi/cpiai.txt
2. http://nhts.ornl.gov/2001/html_files/trends_ver6.shtml
3. http://www.bls.gov/cex/2001/standard/multiyr.pdf for 1993-2001
and http://www.bls.gov/cex/1992/standard/multiyr.pdf for 1984-1992

Note: Shaded cell data estimated from 1983 NPTS data.

household size declining and per household and per capita travel levels increasing. This is a result of a number of factors including the fact that auto travel has relatively high fixed costs and relatively modest variable costs. For example, the Internal Revenue Service had long assumed full costs per VMT of approximately 36 cents and marginal costs of 12 cents for tax deduction purposes. The fixed cost of vehicle ownership results in the marginal cost of additional travel being more modest than one might presume from looking at the total cost per VMT in Table 1.

The fixed cost of travel is predominately related to the cost of the vehicle and the fixed costs of ownership such as insurance and registration. Thus, the actual marginal cost for travel is very modest and may not be meaningfully affected by real income changes in a given household. However, to the extent that real income increases enable additional auto ownership, one might expect jumps in VMT per household or person as a given household passes the real income threshold that enables adding an additional vehicle. The apparent critical consideration in VMT is vehicle availability and, when latent vehicle demand is saturated, the impact of real income growth on travel growth may be dampened.

Real income growth may continue to influence the desire to participate in additional away-from-home activities that require travel, assuming there are no time budget constraints on doing so.

Income growth's influence on travel may have more to do with the ability to afford the activities than the ability to afford the requisite travel in order to participate. The transportation share of the cost of activities such as shopping or entertainment may not be the critical determinant in choosing to travel. Arguably, the importance of real income growth may be lower than in prior decades when auto availability was lower. While there are certainly some low-income households that have resource constraints on travel and auto ownership, the size of this segment of the population is far more modest than has historically been the case. The zero-car household share (approximately 9 percent of households in 2001 versus 20 percent in 1969, according to the NHTS) minimizes the magnitude of the impact that could be realized by declines in the share of zero-car households. Mental and physical health, legal constraints, and chronic financial conditions will continue to preclude some share of the population from ever being able to have autos available. The current 9 percent of households with zero-cars comprise only 5.1 percent of the population.

Figure 16 shows the trends in both real household incomes and in cost per VMT. This cost data was developed by combining data from the national travel surveys (NPTS 1983, 1990, 1995, and NHTS 2001) with information from the Bureau of Labor Statistics on household spending. The upward trend in real household income in spite of a declining household size is readily apparent. Similarly, the downward trend in per-mile vehicle operating costs also is apparent. This trend appears to have flattened and, in fact, shows a slight recent increase. As Figure 16 shows, the real cost of travel, in cost per vehicle mile, has declined and appears to have been relatively stable in the past decade. Declining occupancies offset part of the lower cost per VMT and a plot of expenditure per PMT would show a more stable cost per mile of person travel. It is difficult to predict how future vehicle operating costs will trend. A competitive global auto market and low current interest rates have enabled the capital cost of vehicle ownership to remain modest. Rising but still moderate costs for fuel are unlikely to single-handedly drive

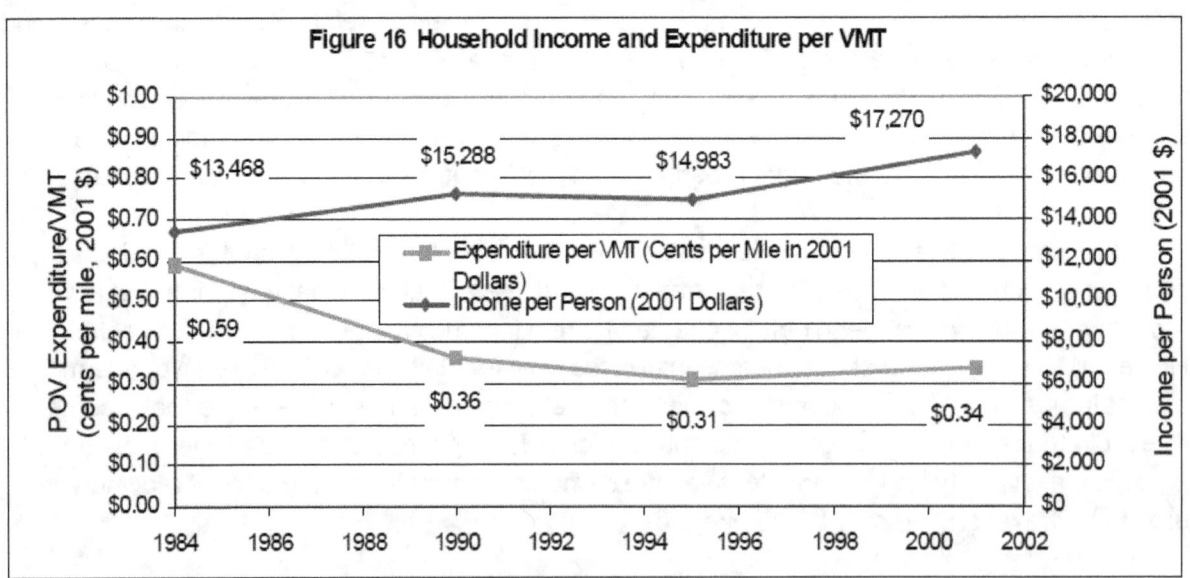

Figure 16 Household Income and Expenditure per VMT

Source: CUTR analysis of NHTS/NPTS data and Bureau of Labor Statistics Consumer Expenditure and Consumer Price Index data.

costs up significantly. Longer-term fuel, parking and insurance costs may accelerate if scarcities of energy, higher land costs, and accelerating medical costs have an impact. The end of the decline in the cost of travel may contribute to a dampening of travel demand growth.

Looking ahead, several considerations suggest that slower growth in household income may occur as labor force participation has stabilized, and the age profile suggests that the share of the population in their peak earning years may now be near a maximum. The critical factor going forward may be the extent to which the economy continues to see productivity gains and the extent to which retirement saving needs and energy and health care costs, for example, impact growth in discretionary income available to spend on activities that require travel.

### Vehicle Availability

As noted, a factor related to travel cost and income is vehicle availability. Figure 17 shows person trip rates as a function of household vehicle availability. The adequacy of vehicle availability was defined based on the relationship between the number of adults and vehicles in the household. Adults are defined in the NHTS database as persons 18 years of age and older. To understand the risk of additional travel demand from growing vehicle availability, it was assumed that each household with a current vehicle shortage (as noted on the right hand side of Figure 17) would have per-person trip-making rates equal to households with no vehicle shortages. Seventy-five percent of the population is in households with no vehicle shortages, as defined above. The increase in trip rates would result in an increase in the total trip making of less than 5 percent. Thus, there is some evidence that even with additional vehicle availability VMT growth would be meaningful but not large in the context of the history of annual increases in overall VMT.

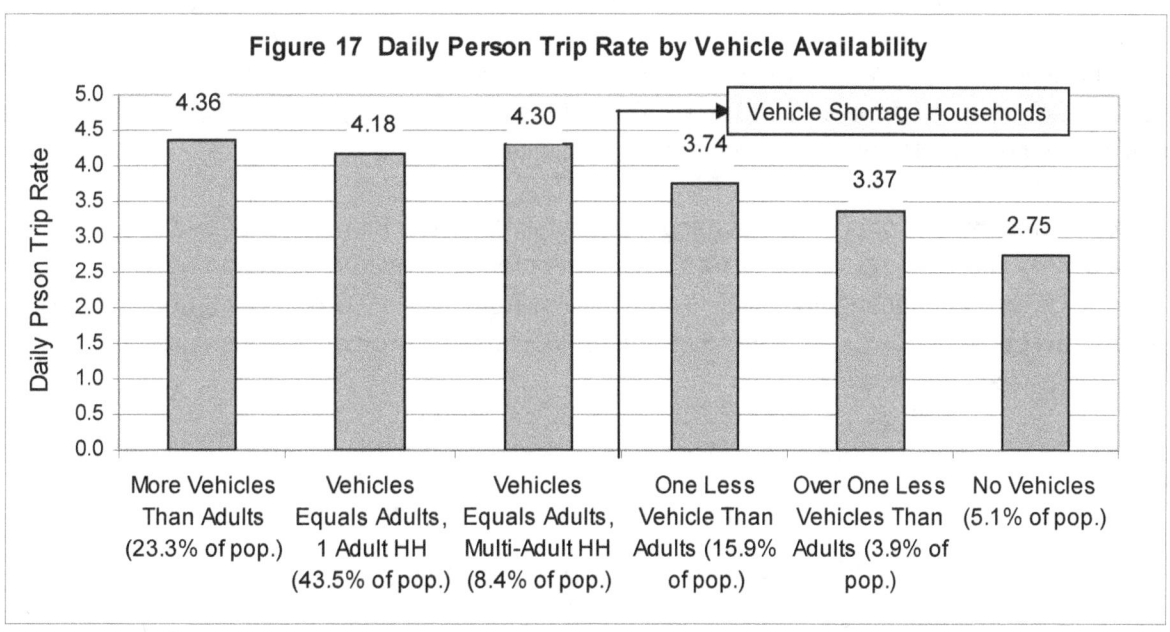

Source: CUTR analysis of 2001 NHTS data.

## Time Use and Travel Time

One of the factors that influence travel is the time resource that people are willing to invest in travel. Historically, individuals have been willing to invest approximately 20 minutes to travel to and from work and additional time to travel for other purposes. Figure 18 shows the trend in journey to work travel time. The 3.1-minute increase in the past decade appears to reflect a combination of longer trips, slower speeds, and changes in coding of the census data[2]. As culture and society norms change the investment of time in travel has also changed. In some instances, phenomena such as commuting longer distances to afford a single-family home have resulted in growing commute time commitments. Far more dramatic has been the phenomenon where individuals have traded off time spent in activities at home for time spent traveling and in activity away from home. Typical of that trend has been the increase in the number of meals eaten or purchased away from home. More

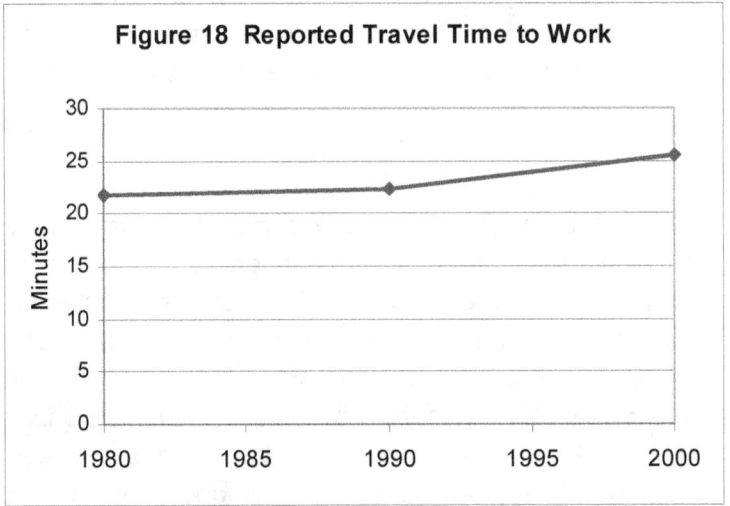

**Figure 18 Reported Travel Time to Work**

Source: Census data.

often households that are smaller with more working members have shown a willingness to, in effect, specialize their labor, working more at their job and using those earnings to purchase services that might have been done by a household member at home in a prior generation. Even technology has played a factor in time use, with cell phones, the Internet, microwaves, disposable diapers, pre-peeled carrots and other household appliances and products resulting in changes in how individuals spend time. The simple fact that household sizes are smaller has significantly reduced the time commitment for family care.

Figure 19 presents national data on changes since 1965 in how individuals spend their time. It is particularly interesting to note that free time has increased, thus providing an opportunity for increased time commitments to travel. The evidence from the NPTS/NHTS suggest that the person travel time budget is far from fixed and, in fact, shows a remarkably consistent growth rate over the past few decades.

---

[2] Trips longer than 99 minutes were truncated in 1990 but not in 2000. Analysis of the 2000 data suggests that this might explain as much of a minute of the increase.

As shown in Figure 20, the minutes per day per person that have been spent on travel have been increasing almost two minutes per person per day per year since 1983. Unlike other trends discussed elsewhere in this report, there is no evidence of a dampening of this trend. While some of this travel time budget increase is no doubt attributable to the changes in average age and the increases in labor force participation and the subsequent economic activity, other factors such as the changes in activity patterns brought about by culture, technology and other changes are most certainly involved. While congestion and the resultant slower speeds may absorb some of this additional travel time, it nonetheless, supports the historic trend of increasing per capita VMT.

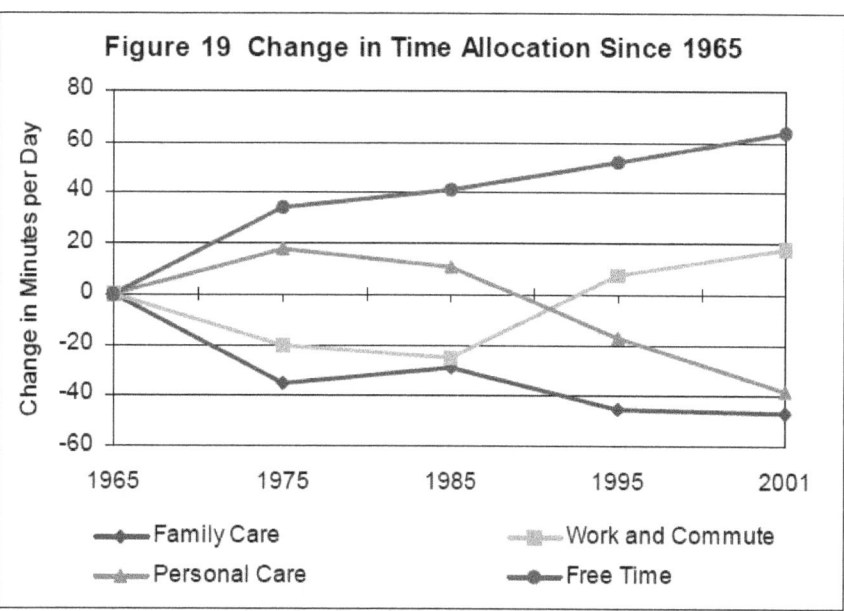

Figure 19  Change in Time Allocation Since 1965

Source: *Americans' Use of Time Project*, cited in Robinson, 1999 and 1998-2001 Time Diary Studies.

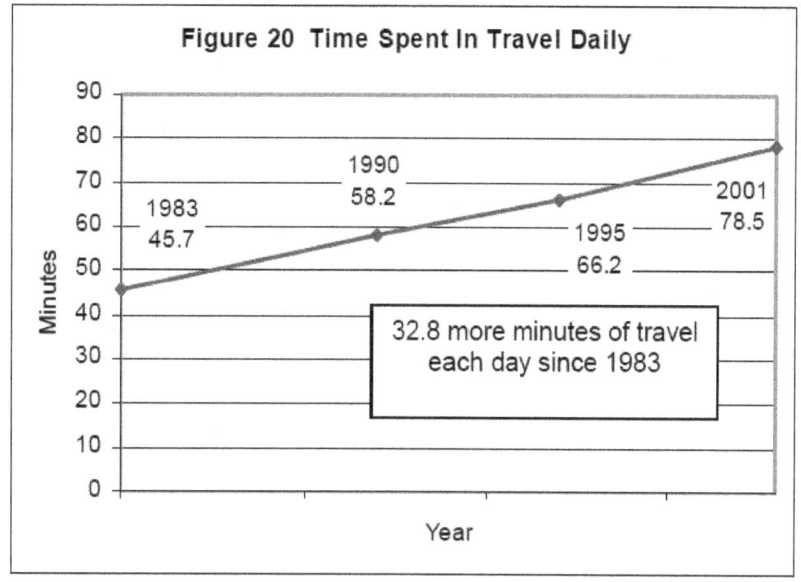

Figure 20  Time Spent In Travel Daily

Source: NHTS/NPTS data.

Figure 21 converts time use trends into annual changes (expressed in minutes per day) in time spent on the activity categories used in the *Americans' Use of Time Project*. This figure adds travel time information from NHTS/NPTS to contrast the change in the amount of time spent on all travel as reported in NHTS/NPTS with changes in time spent on each of the four activity groupings used in the *Americans' Use of Time Project*[3]. The use of annual changes enables comparison of data from different time periods and sources.

---

[3] Note: work commuting time is including in the measure of NHTS/NPTS Travel Time as well as in the Work and Commute time data.

One immediately wonders how sustainable the trend of increases in time spent in travel is. When will other activities deter additional increases in time allocated to travel? It also raises the question as to whether changes in the economy and society that enable larger time commitments to travel will continue. For example, the ability to travel to and purchase a prepared meal at a grocery store or restaurant may be more time efficient than preparing a comparable meal at home. The presence and frequent use of cell

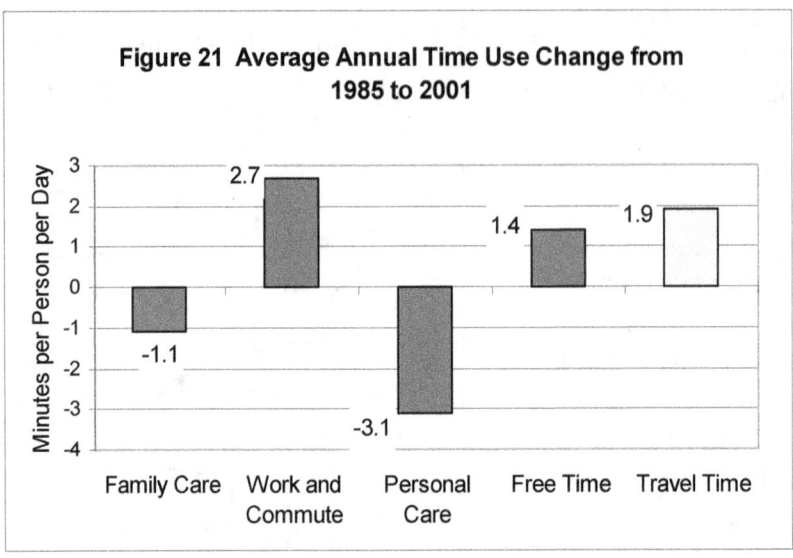

Source: Source: *Americans' Use of Time Project* cited in Robinson, 1999 and 1998-2001 Time Diary Studies, and NHTS/NPTS analysis.

phones by travelers may be another example of how travel time is being used as multitask time. Hence, growth in travel time budgets may not be as onerous as once thought. Reducing the stress of travel delay by communicating via cell phone may minimize the onerousness of vehicle travel. Eating and drinking, books on tape, and unfortunately, other activities are commonly carried out during vehicle travel. The ability to multitask may minimize the desire to limit travel time. Work trip travel time has been historically quite stable; however, even commute time appears to be experiencing upward pressure based on 2000 census data. It appears that housing affordability will continue to force longer commutes for some segments of the population.

## LAND USE INFLUENCES ON TRAVEL

While this report focuses predominately on socio-economic considerations and revealed changes in travel behavior — travel behavior and future travel demand cannot be discussed without acknowledging the role of land use. The relationship between land use and transportation pre-dates recorded history as transportation corridors on both land and sea influenced the course of development and commerce. The more contemporary recognition of the relationship between land use and transportation demand dates back several decades and has long been recognized as a critical relationship by transportation planners.

The consequences of various urban development and design strategies and the configuration of the transportation network have been of interest for several decades as the profession has become more sensitive to the relationship between transportation and land use. In the 1970's, there were several initiatives to understand this relationship from the perspective of understanding the energy use implications of various urban development and transportation network patterns. The classic 1989 article, "Gasoline Consumption and Cities," by Kenworthy and Newman in the *Journal of the American Planning Association*, provided empirical data on comparative energy use for various urban areas across the globe (Kenworthy and Newman 1989). The original "Cost of Sprawl" study by the Real Estate Research Corporation (1974) initiated the now lengthy and ongoing discussions of the cost of sprawl, where the infrastructure and operating costs of services required for various development patterns, especially of transportation, are compared. The 1990's in particular saw a heightened interest in the relationship between urban form and transportation needs. The growing investment in transit systems, increasing levels of congestion, concerns about global warming and "paving over the environment," and unwillingness or inability to identify acceptable transportation investments and adequate resource commitments to keep pace with growing travel demand heightened interest in longer term development and design solutions for moderating the growth of travel demand. *Travel by Design, The Influence of Urban Form on Travel*, speaks to the continuing interest in the topic (Boarnet and Crane 2001). This comprehensive review goes a long way toward characterizing the state of knowledge in a book length document.

In perhaps the most comprehensive synthesis of research on the effects of land use traits on transportation, TRCP Report 95, Chapter 15, *Land Use and Site Design, Traveler Response to Transportation System Changes,* provides a comprehensive overview of the research results with particular attention to discerning quantitative measures of the relationships (Transportation Research Board 2003). The major variables describing land use that were used as a basis for organizing the findings were density, diversity (mix of uses), and design. The report provides a powerful perspective on both the complexity of the subject and research challenges associated with defining, quantifying, and disaggregating the numerous factors that collectively influence travel behavior as well as on the current state of knowledge as it relates to quantifiable relationships between travel and the subject land use traits.

While there remains a great deal of uncertainty regarding the magnitude of the influence of various land use characteristics on travel demand and the transferability of experiences in one location to other locations or populations, there is a shared understanding of the basics of how land use influences the demand for travel. Figure 22 characterizes the basic relationships. Greater accessibility is a condition associated with the land use traits of higher development density, a mix of land uses, better connectivity of the transportation network, attractive urban design that enables safe and convenient mobility, activity scale in proportion to the community scale, and contiguous development. Greater accessibility has the affects on VMT as noted in Figure 22. Trip making would be expected to increase in highly accessible areas. Alone this would increase total travel demand. However, accessibility is also likely to produce shorter trips and may enable easier trip linking due to closer proximity of potential destinations and a well-connected (more direct) travel network. In addition, mode selection would be more likely to enable or favor non-auto modes. Thus, the composite affect on person travel or vehicle travel would be the product of these impacts. It is generally observed that greater accessibility associated with better transportation-land use coordination will result in lower VMT.

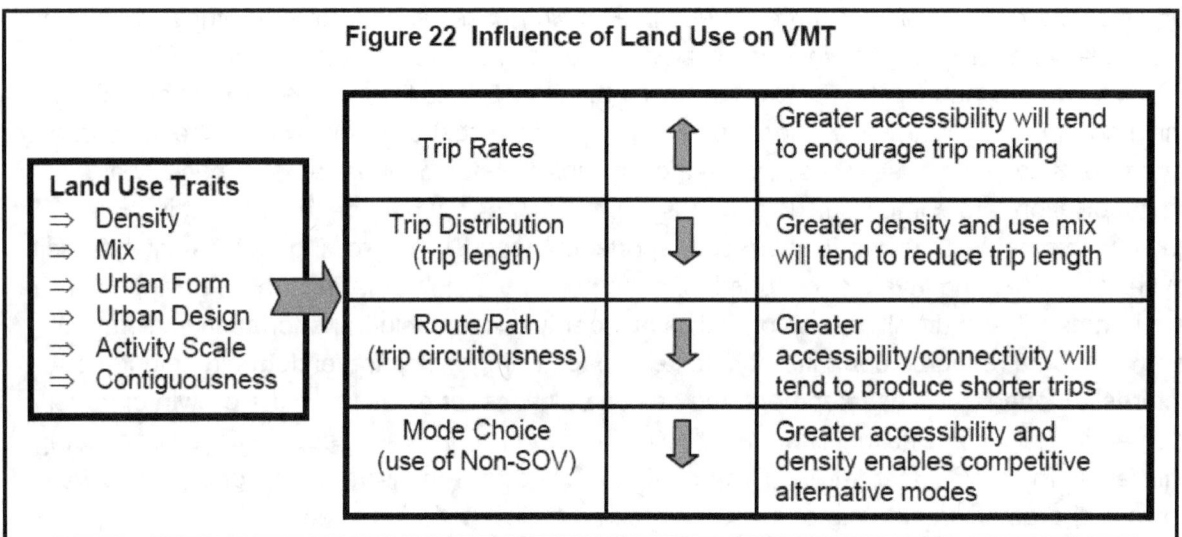

**Figure 22 Influence of Land Use on VMT**

In time, the presence of powerful Geographic Information System (GIS) analysis tools and greater precision in defining land use characteristics are likely to produce a refined understanding of the empirical relationship between land use and travel and enable researchers to monitor the relationship over time. At present, such longitudinal data with sufficient precision are unavailable and researchers are less able to discern the relative impacts of land use from the other impacts such as changes in socio-economic conditions as noted earlier.

## TRANSPORTATION SYSTEM INFLUENCE ON TRAVEL

Travel is subject to the basic supply-demand principles that govern consumption of virtually all products and services. Thus, it would be expected that the performance of the transportation system would influence the demand for travel. The performance of the system includes considerations such as speed or adequacy of capacity, safety, reliability, cost, comfort etc. As noted in the discussion of socio-economic factors, travel cost and vehicle availability are among the transportation system characteristics that are known to be factors influencing VMT. Other factors such as safety and convenience are admittedly important, but their relationship to travel demand is less well understood. The adequacy of capacity as it impacts delay (or speed), and reliability of travel are perhaps the most significant performance characteristics in terms of impacting VMT. One of the critical factors in enabling growth in VMT has been the change in speed of travel. Unfortunately, national average system speed is one of the most difficult data items to attain as there are limited sources for data about average travel speed. Historically, auto travel speeds have been increasing despite the fact that speeds on individual facilities have been falling. Higher attained speeds have been realized due to shifts to higher classification roadway facilities and more rapid growth in volumes on higher speed roadways.

Figure 23 shows the change in the share of traffic on various facility types over time and identifies the large increase in freeway facility share. Other factors include shifts from the peak to the off-peak travel period, shifts from congested urban to less congested suburban facilities, and changes to faster modes such as single occupant vehicle (SOV) versus walk, transit, and carpooling. Thus, the combined effect of these changes has enabled travel speeds to increase over time.

One of the critical constraints on future VMT growth could be the fact that system speeds are no longer increasing and appear to be declining. As indicated in prior sections of this report, many of the conditions that have enabled faster travel, such as mode shifts, appear to have run their course. Combined with the increasing congestion levels and resource constraints for increasing system capacity, it is anticipated that congestion levels will continue to produce slower travel speeds.

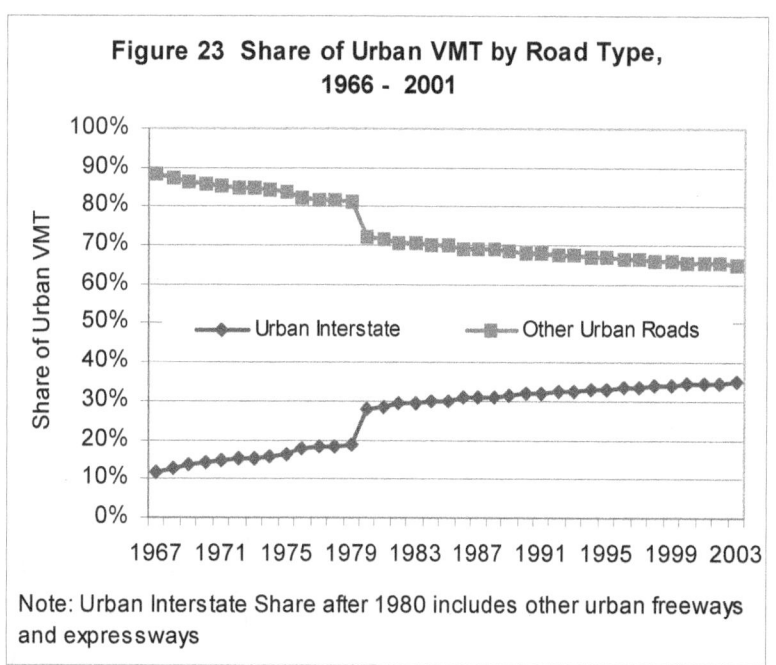

Figure 23 Share of Urban VMT by Road Type, 1966 - 2001

Note: Urban Interstate Share after 1980 includes other urban freeways and expressways

Source: FHWA Highway Statistics data.

---

Figure 24 shows the average reported travel speeds for respondents in the national household surveys. This set of data, for work trips and all trips, confirms slowing attained speeds in the past decade and suggests that the decline in speeds is accelerating. If a constant or at least modestly growing travel time budget is presumed, then slower speeds may result in less total VMT. The reversal of trend in attained travel speeds may be more significant than the trends in some of the other socio-demographic variables and mode choice considerations in terms of future VMT levels. The multi-

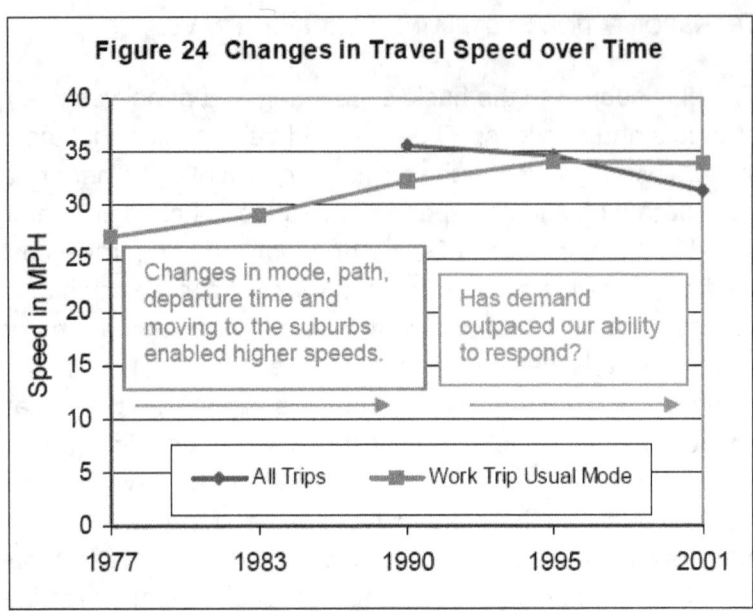

Source: CUTR analysis of NHTS/NPTS data.

decade trend of increasing travel speed has enabled growth in VMT independent of increases in the time spent in travel. Going forward, it is likely that this historic inducement to greater VMT will disappear or be replaced with a drag impact on VMT growth if worsening congestion levels result in declines in travel speeds as are forecasted in many urban areas.

## DIRECT DRIVERS OF TRAVEL BEHAVIOR

The direct drivers of travel demand are the population, trip rates, trip length and mode choice. These factors are influenced by the phenomenon discussed earlier but can be more directly traced to the level of travel demand. Each of these elements is discussed below.

### Population as a Contributor to VMT Growth

Between 1977 and 2001, the U.S. population increased by 30 percent, from 213 million to 277 million persons. While the 30 percent increase is a significant contributor to travel demand growth, it is not the most significant factor in VMT growth in this time period.

### Trip Rates as a Contributor to VMT Growth

The historical changes in trip length and trip rates over the past 24 years are shown in Figure 25. In the 1977 to 2001 time period, per capita trip rates increased by 49 percent. A small part of this increase may be explained by survey method changes, including more aggressively capturing non-vehicle trips in the database and more aggressive diary and phone follow-ups. However, this does not take away from the obviously very large increase in trip making. Trip rate increases is the single largest contributor to travel growth and a factor that appears to be closely tied to socio-demographic, economic, and cultural conditions as opposed to land use or transportation system characteristics.

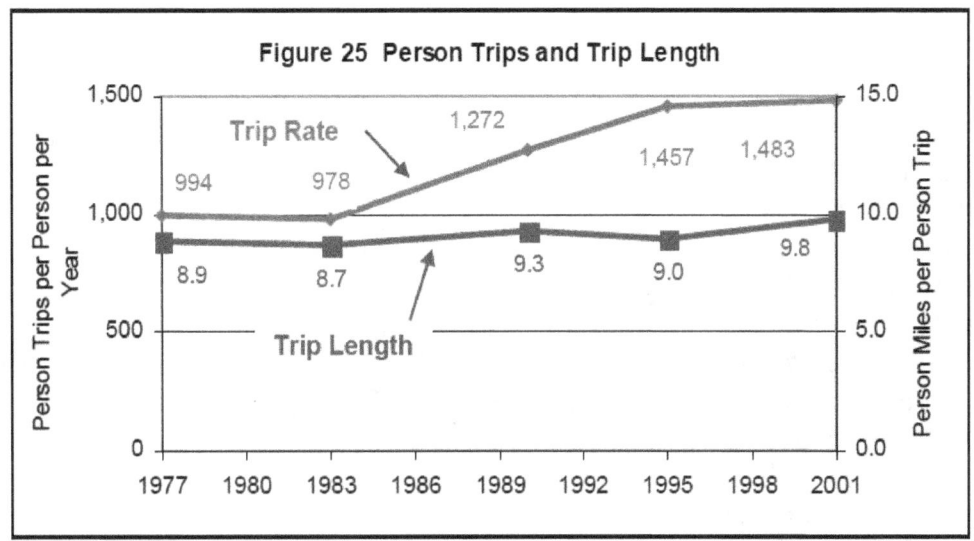

Source: CUTR analysis of NHTS/NPTS.

### Trip Length as a Contributor to VMT Growth

Trip length can be measured in terms of person miles of travel per person trip. Trip length for all trips has increased from slightly less than 9 miles to slightly less than 10 miles in the reference time period, consistent with the expectations that suburbanization has resulted in longer trip lengths. This ten percent increase partially explains increases in VMT. More aggressive sampling of walk and bike trips in the data collection effort in more recent years may have also dampened the measured trip length increase by including more of these short trips in the sample. Trip chaining may also be moderating the pace of growth in trip length. In the time period of reference, trip length experienced the lowest percent increase of the direct factors contributing to travel demand.

### *Mode Shifts as a Contributor to VMT Growth*

One of the sources for growth in VMT in recent decades has been the shift to drive alone as a mode or single occupant vehicle (SOV) travel. Over the past few decades, this shift has contributed to the growth in VMT. However, as the information below hypothesizes, mode shifts are less likely to be a contributor to future VMT growth. Changes in shares for each of the non-SOV modes are discussed below.

#### *Walking Mode Share*

Part of the mode shift change is the decline in walking. While walk trips are shorter and modest in share, they characterize the historic decline in non-POV modes. Figure 26 shows the change in walking to work. Recent improvements in data collection have increased the reporting of

other walk trips, many of which are for exercise and walking the dogs. However, the work trip walk mode share indicates one of the functional uses of the walking mode and portrays the decline. The data suggest that the declining trend may have ended or reversed in the mid-1990s. The limited time frame for data and survey method changes make it premature to reach a firm conclusion at this point in time. However, it is clear that the possibility for additional declines is limited by the

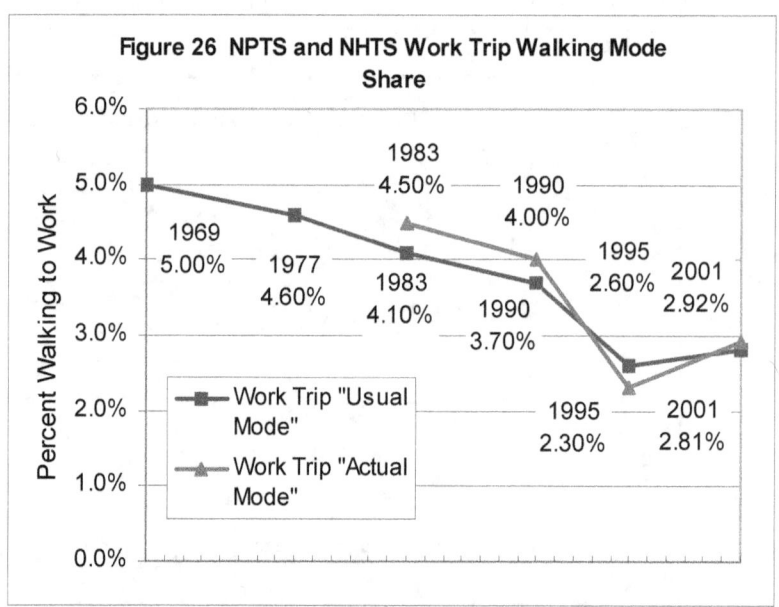

Source: CUTR analysis of NHTS/NPTS data.

modest shares that continue to use walking for work trips. Figure 27 reports walk mode share as reported by the Census. The consistency between the Census and NHTS for 1990 and 2000/2001 is encouraging.

*Transit Mode Share*

Similar analysis of the transit mode share has been done by Polzin and Chu (2003). Figure 28 presents the results of several survey sources that produce measures of transit mode share based on the percentage of person trips by transit. These measures indicate a historic decline in transit mode share with some evidence of stabilization or perhaps a slight increase in transit share more recently. The Census data on commute modes, for example, shows transit

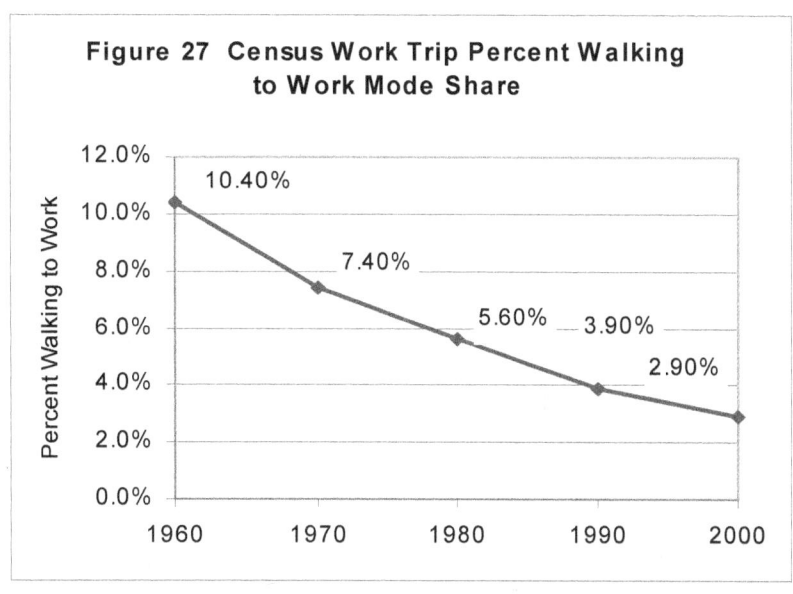

Source: Census data.

shares declining from 8.90 percent in 1970 to 4.70 percent in 2000. The lowest series of points in Figure 28 is NHTS/NPTS data for all trips, not just work trips. This data shows transit mode

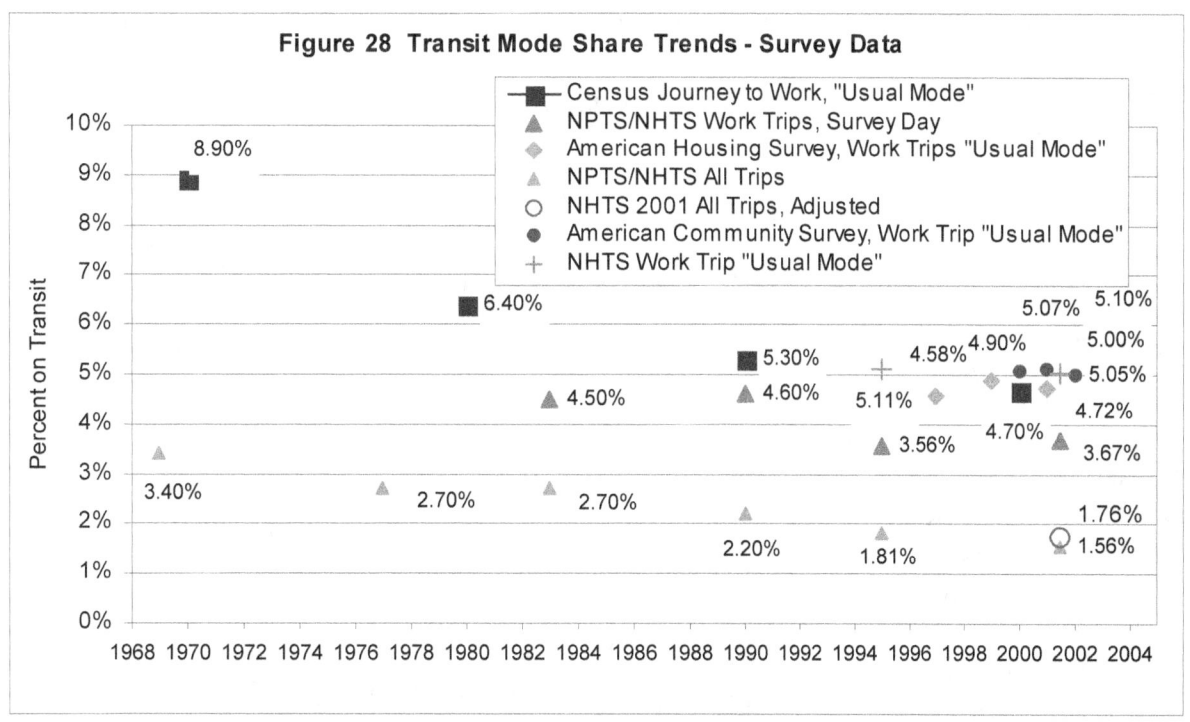

Source: CUTR analysis of various Census and NHTS/NPTS data sources.

---

shares declining from 3.40 percent in 1969 to 1.56 percent in 2001[4]. There are variations in survey methods, definitions, and sample sizes among the data sources; however, the composite picture gives a strong perspective on the overall trends.

Figure 29 is a calculated mode share based on person miles of travel (as opposed to trips). This figure, derived from national VMT and transit ridership data and expressed in terms of person miles of travel, also shows a turn in the trend of transit mode share declines. Even if this reversal of trend is not sustained over time, it appears that the rate of decline in transit use has been reduced and future shifts from transit are not likely to be a significant contributor to future growth in VMT. The low share of transit use limits the possible impact on VMT of declining transit use. Even if all transit disappeared - a virtually impossible outcome - the impact on aggregate VMT would be limited to less than two percent.

*Carpooling*

The final area of changes in mode share relate to changes in vehicle occupancies. This is sometimes referred to as changes in auto occupancies, changes in passenger shares, or carpooling shares. Regardless of the terminology used, it refers to the share of

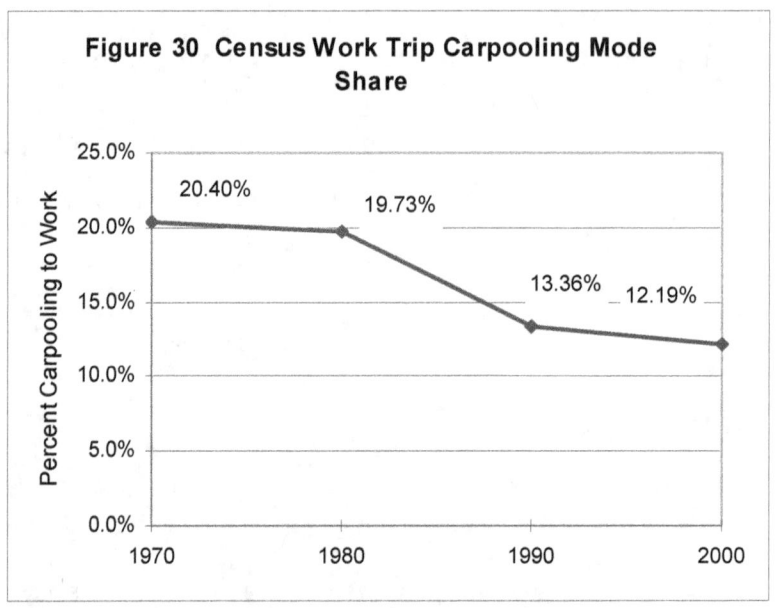

**Figure 29  Urban Public Transportation Mode Share Based Person Miles of Travel**

Source: CUTR analysis of VMT, NTD, and NHTS/NPTS data.

**Figure 30  Census Work Trip Carpooling Mode Share**

Source: CUTR analysis of NHTS/NPTS data.

---

[4] Adjustments to the raw 2001 NHTS transit mode share number to make it more consistent with prior NPTS surveys increases the transit mode share from 1.56% to 1.76%.

travelers that are traveling as passengers in an auto.

Figure 30 shows the carpool share as reported in census journey-to-work data. The substantial decline matches conventional wisdom as more dispersed travel patterns and greater auto availability have contributed to a higher share of drive-alone work trips.

Figure 31 shows the reported vehicle occupancies for work and all trips based on the national surveys. Both series of data suggest a stabilization of the trip occupancy. With average household size stabilizing and the work trip mode share already very low, there is limited opportunity for additional declines in occupancies. Social conventions are likely to continue to result in multi-

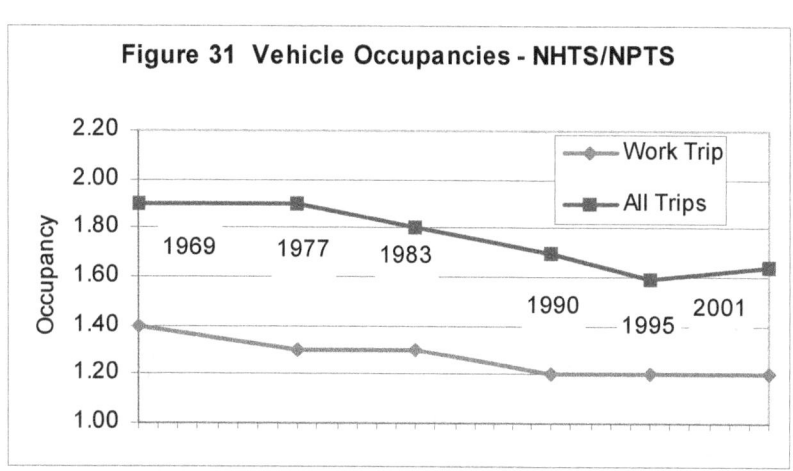

Source: CUTR analysis of NHTS/NPTS data.

occupant social and recreational trip purposes. For example, child chauffeuring and many social trips will remain multi-occupant trips. Thus, the potential for further declines in occupancies contributing to VMT growth are more limited than has historically been the case.

Figure 32 shows the ratio of vehicle miles of travel to person mile of travel from the NPTS/NHTS data series. This measure captures the aggregate affect of the mode use on vehicle miles of travel. Increases in VMT/PMT indicate more people are traveling in SOVs rather than as passengers, transit users, or walkers and bikers. As this graphic indicates, between 1977 and 1995 there were increases in the VMT/PMT ratio. This is consistent with declines in walking, transit use, and shared ride travel during that period. The shift in curve direction in 1995 is believed to reflect a combination of factors, including the stabilizations or reversals of modal use trends and the fact that the 2001 survey was far more aggressive in capturing non-VMT trips, including walk and bike trips and trips by persons under age 5. These data indicate that the changes in mode contribute to an increase of 25.5

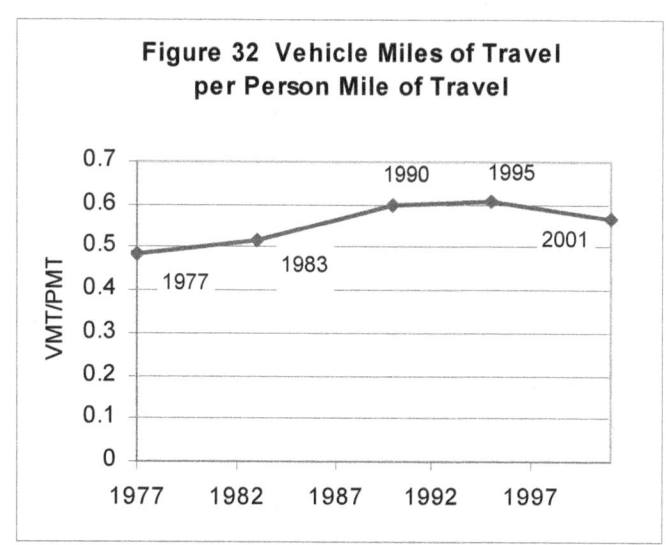

Source: CUTR analysis of NHTS/NPTS data.

percent in VMT between 1977 and 1995 or approximately 17.4 percent if measured between 1977 and 2001.

Figure 33 provides a graphic representation of the percentage change in factors that contribute to VMT growth between 1977 and 2001.

Figure 34 shows the cumulative impact of the various factors that directly influence VMT in terms of the

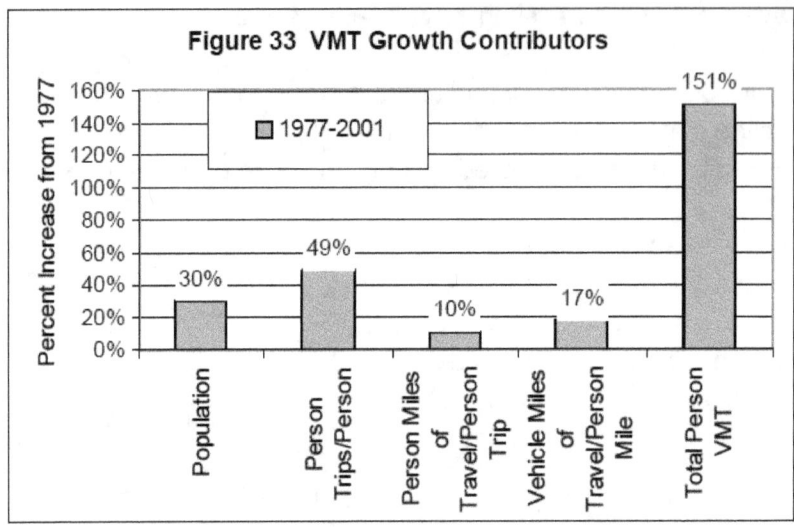

Source:  CUTR analysis with NHTS/NPTS.

percent that each factor contributes to the increase in person VMT in the 1977 to 2001 period. For example, had per capita trip frequency remained the same, VMT would have only grown approximately half as much.  Perhaps the most surprising result of Figure 34 is the significance of trip frequency in explaining overall travel growth and, in contrast, the relatively modest contribution of trip length increases.

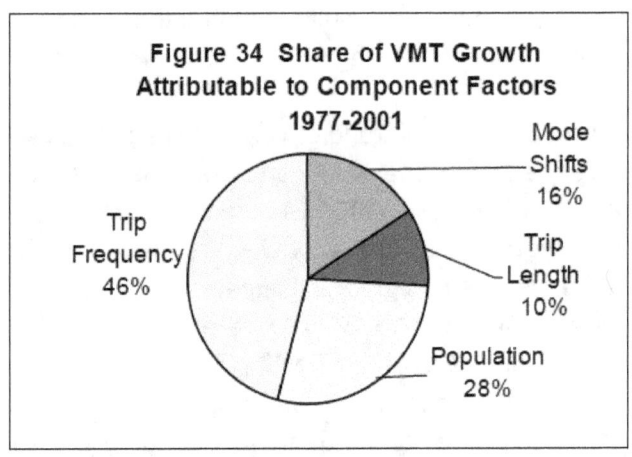

Source:  CUTR analysis of NHTS/NPTS data.

## VMT Growth

By using historic data on travel behavior from the Nationwide Personal Transportation Surveys (NPTS) and the National Household Travel Survey (NHTS), an understanding of the relative significance of various factors in contributing to the increase in person VMT as measured by these surveys can be gleaned. These factors disaggregate growth in VMT into the terms commonly referred to as population, trip rate, trip length, and mode choice. The growth in VMT can be characterized as the product of these factors, as shown in the formula below. This particular formula was selected because each of the components can be evaluated with empirical data and the components are comprehensible in terms familiar to planners and the general public.

$$\text{Formula 1.)} \quad \text{Population} \times \underbrace{\frac{\text{Person Trips}}{\text{Person}}}_{(trip\ rate)} \times \underbrace{\frac{\text{Person Miles}}{\text{Person Trip}}}_{(trip\ length)} \times \underbrace{\frac{\text{Vehicle Miles}}{\text{Person Mile}}}_{(mode\ choice)} = \text{Vehicle Miles of Travel}$$

These components are synonymous with the traditional four-step process often used by transportation professionals to model travel.

Table 2 includes NHTS and NPTS data for these factors and other key metrics between 1977 and 2001. The shaded cells in the right hand column in Table 2 are the percent changes for the factors used in Formula 1. Each is discussed below.

### Table 2  Summary NPTS and NHTS Data and Key Indicators

| | 1977 | 1983 | 1990 | 1990 adjusted | 1995 | 2001 | Percent Change 1977 to 2001 |
|---|---|---|---|---|---|---|---|
| Population | 213,141 | 229,453 | 239,416 | 239,416 | 259,994 | 277,208 | 30.06% |
| Household Vehicle Trips (000,000) | 108,826 | 126,874 | 158,927 | 193,916 | 229,745 | 234,994 | 115.94% |
| Household VMT (000,000) | 907,603 | 1,002,139 | 1,409,600 | 1,695,290 | 2,068,368 | 2,281,863 | 151.42% |
| Person Trips (000,000) | 211,778 | 224,385 | 249,562 | 304,471 | 378,930 | 410,969 | 94.06% |
| Person Miles of Travel (000,000) | 1,879,215 | 1,946,662 | 2,315,300 | 2,829,936 | 3,411,122 | 4,026,158 | 114.25% |
| Person Trips Per Person Per Year (trip rate) | 994 | 978 | 1042 | 1272 | 1457 | 1483 | 49.21% |
| Person Miles of Travel Per Person Trip (trip length) | 8.874 | 8.676 | 9.277 | 9.295 | 9.002 | 9.797 | 10.40% |
| Vehicle Miles of Travel Per Person Mile (mode choice) | 0.483 | 0.515 | 0.609 | 0.599 | 0.606 | 0.567 | 17.35% |

Source:  FHWA NPTS/NHTS Summary table with CUTR Calculations.
Note: 1990 data was adjusted for methodological differences.

A second formula is also used to explore travel behavior changes. This formula similarly enables the exploration and forecasting of future travel by using estimates of the component variables in a forecast.

$$\text{Formula 2.)} \quad \text{Population} \times \frac{\text{Person Hours}}{\text{Person}} \times \frac{\text{Vehicle Miles}}{\text{Person Hour}} = \text{Vehicle Miles of Travel}$$

### VMT Growth by 2025

Given the exploration of the growth in VMT it is logical to speculate on the implications for the future. This is not intended to be a rigorous empirical forecast but rather an educated estimate informed by knowledge of evolving trends in various travel behavior characteristics. This report uses two simple formulas to forecast VMT growth. Utilizing the formulas for VMT growth, it can be speculated what might be the expected change in each component factor. In both formulas each component is expressed in terms of percent change over current conditions. The base period for comparison is the 1977 to 2001 period of 24 years. These dates coincide with NHTS/NPTS survey dates. Conveniently, forecasting forward 24 years takes one to 2025, the time horizon for many long range plans and a useful reference point.

Population – Common to both formulas is an estimate of population. This is taken from published Census sources. Population is forecast to increase 22 percent between 2001 and 2025, according to the Bureau of Census mid-level forecasts. This pace of growth in slower in percentage terms than the prior 24 years.

Trip Rate – Used in Formula 1, trip making had been a major contributor to VMT growth. This has been driven by a host of socio-economic considerations including female labor force participation, real income increases, smaller household sizes, and the age profile of the population. These trends may have substantially played themselves out and, going forward, travel behavior is likely to change more slowly. It is postulated that the rate of trip making per capita will grow at about a third the rate in the past twenty-four years, resulting in a 16 percent increase over the time period.

Trip Length – Used in Formula 1, trip length is partially influenced by dispersion of activities, to some extent by trip chaining rates, and to some extent by the specialization of labor and activities that influences how far one might have to travel, for example, to visit a doctor. Trip length growth has been relatively modest and is postulated to remain modest with growth of 8 percent by 2025 versus 10 percent over the past 18 years. Growing congestion levels are expected to constrain the growth in trip length as is the trend toward dispersion of non-home trips ends throughout urban areas. However, appreciating housing prices, higher home ownership rates (which tend to result in more stable home locations), and the high cost of moving to reduce commute travel, may contribute to longer commutes.

Mode Choice – Used in Formula 1, mode choice trends influence VMT when travelers shift more trips to or from single occupant vehicles. Based on mode change trends, it is assumed that there will only be very modest increases in VMT per PMT attributable to mode changes. It is not possible to replicate the prior twenty-four years' shift to auto travel as the non-auto mode shares are too modest to enable that magnitude of shift to be repeated. Certain segments of the population may be afforded the opportunity for more individual vehicle travel, but modest existing levels of shared ride, walk, and transit travel will minimize the change in VMT resulting from further declines in non-single occupant vehicle travel. It is postulated that the VMT per PMT level will increase only 5 percent over the referenced time period – an amount that would accommodate very modest reductions in transit, walk, and shared ride travel. Very high energy prices or shortages, health concerns that motivate walk and bike modes, or increased concentration of population in areas more conducive to non-auto modes could enable stable or increasing non-auto mode shares.

Travel Time Budget – Used in Formula 2, person hours of travel per person is a measure of the time spent in travel. While trends do not suggest that there is a dampening of this trend yet, socio-demographic changes and resource constraints are such that it is unlikely that this growth trend can be sustained for an additional 24 years. Based on Figure 21, person travel time is increasing at 1.9 minutes per year. If this trend continued, by 2025 it would result in an increase of the travel time per capita to 124 minutes per person per day. While vehicle amenities and multitasking while driving, such as cell phone use, may have lessened the burdensomeness of travel time, it is considered prudent to assume that per person travel time would grow 35 percent in the next 24 years, in contrast to the 68 percent growth in the 24 year period to 2001. This would result in the travel time budget increasing from 78.5 minutes per person per day to approximately 106 minutes per person per day.

Vehicle Miles per Person Hour – Used in Formula 2, vehicle miles per person hour is a composite measure that captures both vehicle speed and mode selection characteristics by reporting vehicle miles of travel per unit of time spent traveling by any mode (time spent walking for example does not increase vehicle miles). Historical data for this measure is shown in Figure 35. Assuming this change in trend is sustained, a decline in vehicle miles of travel per hour spent traveling might be expected. Given the evidence of slowing overall travel speeds and moderating declines or stabilization in non-single occupant auto travel, it is assumed that VMT per person hour will decline 8 percent in the next 24 years. Interestingly, this number is consistent with an informal review of a small sample of metro area travel network speed forecasts for 2025 design year transportation plans.

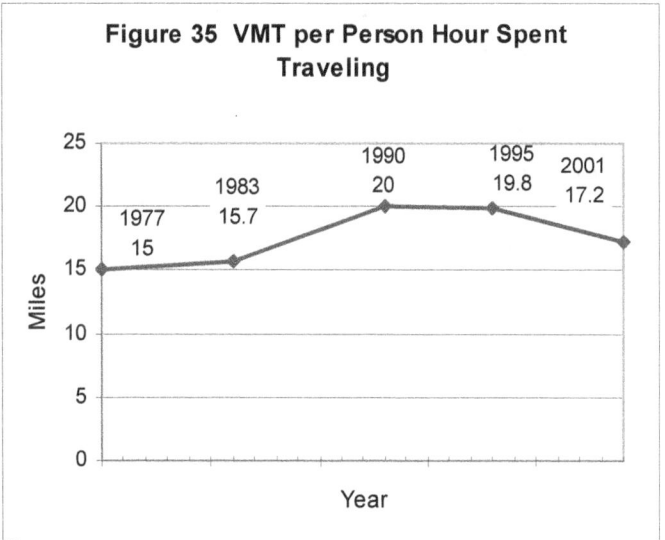

Figure 35  VMT per Person Hour Spent Traveling

Source: CUTR analysis of NHTS/NPTS data.

**Forecast Results**

The results of the two formula applications are presented in Figures 36 and 37. Formula 1, with the given assumptions, produces a total growth in VMT of 60 percent. Formula 2 produces an estimate of increased VMT of 51 percent. The 60 percent increase is approximately 2 percent per year, a level below historical averages but above the levels in three of the last four years and significant in absolute terms and in terms of the need to expand capacity to accommodate demand. The 51 percent increase is the equivalent of 1.74 percent per year, slightly more modest.

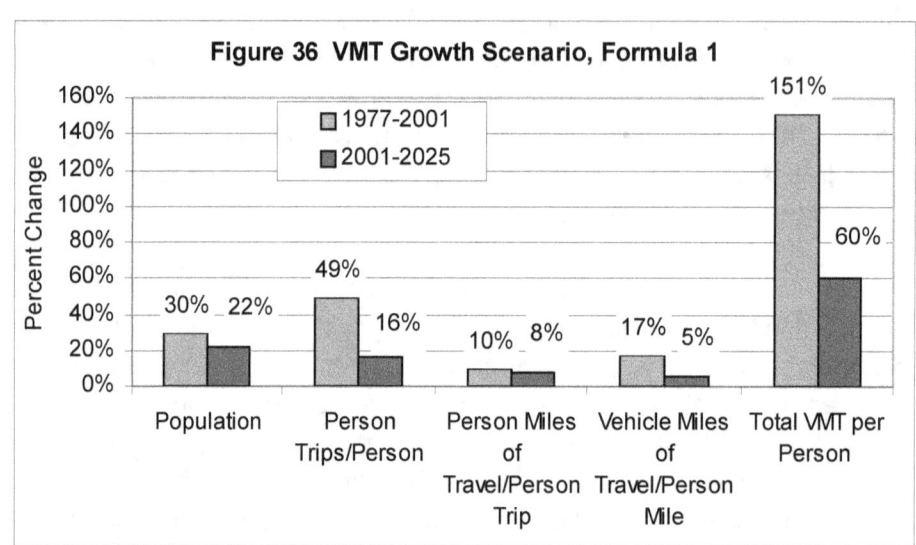

Source: CUTR analysis with NHTS/NPTS.

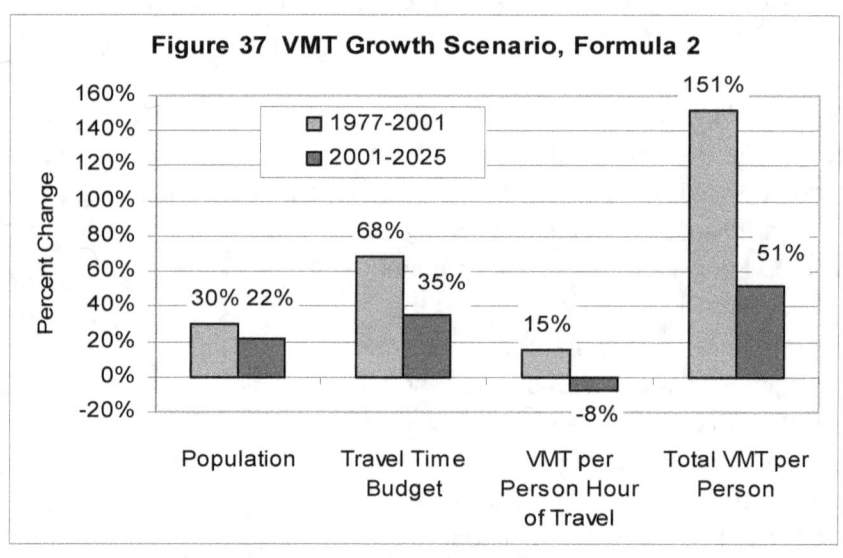

Source: CUTR analysis with NHTS/NPTS.

POLICY IMPLICATIONS

These two scenarios produce estimates that approximate 2 percent per year increases in VMT over the next few decades. These rates of growth are meaningfully below historical levels but consistent with the direction of current trends. Yet each forecast, when looking at the components, raises some interesting policy issues. In the first scenario, the issue of the rate of growth in trip length would appear to be perhaps the most uncertain element in making estimates of future VMT. Will the public be willing to incur additional travel time and money costs for the longer trip lengths that might be implied by the continued outward focused growth patterns or will smart growth type strategies or simply travel behavior priorities preclude significant increases in trip length? Similarly, this scenario assumes a modest additional shift to single occupant vehicles from walk, transit, bike, or shared ride modes. Some might argue that these travel options may, in fact, gain share or at least stabilize at current levels resulting in no additional contribution to VMT increases from mode shifts. There are growing concerns that rapid housing price increases will exacerbate the commute trip length growth as more low and moderate income workers are priced out of the housing market in the areas near their employment. If sustained, this trend could contribute to longer trip lengths.

The second scenario is most remarkable in that it assumes continued strong growth in travel time expenditures per person. The prospect of this trend continuing even at a more moderate pace may seem hard to imagine as, at some point, other activities may preclude additional time being spent on travel. However, international and regional data show a significant variation in person time commitments to travel and there may be structural changes in peoples' time use allocation continuing to take place that enable larger shares of time to be spent in travel.

This scenario also explicitly assumes that travel speeds will be declining. Additional transportation capacity growth beyond historical trends could result if intolerance of slower speeds caused by congestion motivated additional transportation infrastructure investment or if intelligent technologies enabled more rapid growth in capacity of the given roadway network. This issue is addressed in greater detail below.

### Congestion Implications of Future VMT Growth

Perhaps the flaw in the Charles Lave paper referenced previously was the prediction that congestion would not increase due to slowing growth of VMT. While Lave was accurate in terms of the expectations of slowing VMT, he failed to account for the fact that smaller VMT increases may be producing proportionally larger congestion consequences because the speed volume relationship for roadway transportation is not a linear relationship.

Figure 38 shows the classic speed-volume curve as included in the Highway Capacity Manual. This curve, while based on the performance of a single roadway segment, may reflect aggregate roadway system performance to some extent. Thus, this would suggest, depending on which point on the curve from $S_f$ to $D_o$ best represents current aggregate conditions, that more minor increases in flow or demand (moving to the right parallel to the x axis) may be resulting in more significant

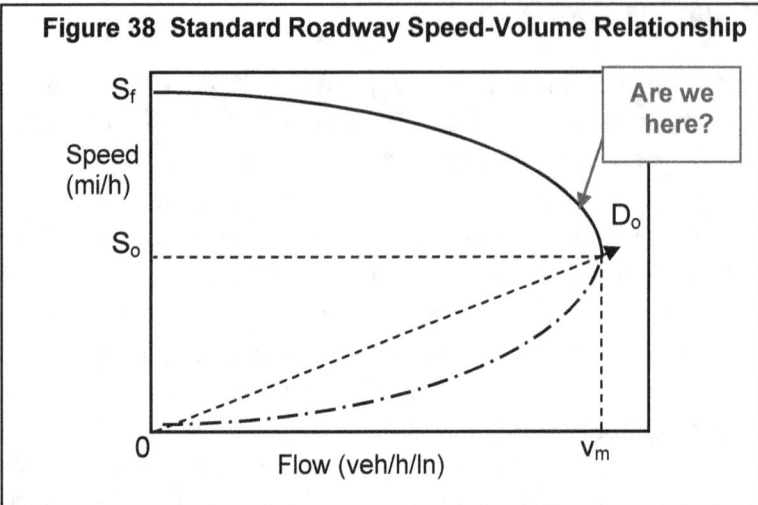

**Figure 38 Standard Roadway Speed-Volume Relationship**

Source: Highway Capacity Manual 2000, Transportation Research Board, National Research Council.

decreases in speed (moving down parallel to the y axis). It suggests that, as the transportation system or at least the urban transportation system approaches high volumes that it is more fragile and more minor increases in demand may be producing as large or larger responses in terms of increased congestion or slowed speed.

If the roadway system is, in fact, more fragile with less reserve capacity and, more likely to be negatively impacted with each marginal increase in roadway volume, it is tempting to speculate on just how the system will respond to additional demand. Obviously, the reaction in terms of system performance will be a feedback factor influencing future demand.

Based on the acceleration of congestion as documented in the Texas Transportation Institute's Urban Mobility Reports (The Annual Urban Mobility Report 2005) and the evidence of slowing travel speeds, one would anticipate these resultant slower speeds placing pressure on roadway volumes. Perhaps more relevant, it encourages speculation on how the roadway system is likely to perform in the future if subjected to the levels of demand that are presumed in this report. While such analyses are implicitly carried out as each urban area prepares their long-range transportation plan, there has been less quantification of this impact at the national level.

Unfortunately, the expectations of moderating VMT growth in percentage or absolute terms offer little relief, if the resultant response of the system is more significant with every incremental increase in demand. The composite impact may be continued deterioration in travel speeds absent a behavioral response in either travel behavior trends or in the public's willingness to politically and financially commit to capacity expansion beyond the record of the recent past.

SUMMARY

Mobility, congestion, transportation infrastructure financing, the role of public transportation, the role of land use, and numerous other topics fundamental to our quality of life have gained an audience beyond the transportation planning profession. The ability of the transportation planning profession to be responsive to policy questions is inherently related to how well the fundamentals of transportation demand and travel behavior are understood.

This report presents evidence that several historic trends appear to have moderated or perhaps changed direction in the past decade and, these may have significant impacts on future VMT growth. Among the direct trends are the mode choice shares for passengers, transit users, and walking. In addition, average travel speed appears to have peaked and may be beginning to slow, a trend that could put pressure on the pace of growing VMT. The report also reviewed a number of the underlying socio-demographic trends that have supported growing VMT. These trends provide strong logical underpinnings to substantiate the causes of the resultant changes in travel behavior that are being observed, many of which appear to be at critical juncture points. Among the trends that may have played themselves out are female labor force participation, household vehicle availability, household size, and female licensure rates. The historic decline in the cost of vehicle travel may also be over.

Collectively, this body of data provides a compelling case for anticipating that VMT growth is moderating. However, unanticipated phenomena such as the apparent unrelenting growth in travel time budgets and growing trips lengths may offset some of the factors that would appear to dampen VMT growth pressures. The report also suggests that planners are not particularly confident in the ability to predict to how the aggregate roadway system will perform when faced with future levels of demand. The premise that the reserve capacity in our system has been nearly fully absorbed and travelers have made the easy adjustments in travel departure times and route choices to utilize the high performing roadway segments, suggests that subsequent increases in demand may result in proportionally more severe consequences in terms of congestion levels and declining speeds. The relatively modest scheduled increases in system capacity expansion compared to demand growth may change if public will and financial support increase. As ever larger shares of a modest transportation trust fund are required to maintain the existing system and accommodate priorities such as safety improvements, the share of resources remaining for operational improvements and capacity expansion may fall further behind and further heighten the sensitivity of the system to increases in demand. Much remains to be seen.

This report identifies a host of potentially significant unknowns that ultimately will influence future travel. Many of these have been long acknowledged as critical policy issues that will influence the future performance of our transportation system. Others indicate potentially new research needs and topics for policy analysis. While there may be more modest VMT growth in the future, there certainly will not be any shortage of transportation challenges and opportunities as professionals strive to understand, forecast, plan for, and deliver transportation infrastructure and services to meet the traveling public's needs.  The set of factors that have influenced travel behavior and demand in the past may be changing and our ability to understand which factors are critical in driving future travel demand will impact our ability to predict and respond to traveler needs.  Understanding long-range travel demands will remain critically important.

## REFERENCES

Boarnet, Marlon G. and Randall Crane. 2001. *Travel by Design, The Influence of Urban Form on Travel.* United Kingdom: Oxford University Press.

Bush, Sarah. 2003. Forecasting 65+ Travel: An Integration of Cohort Analysis and Travel Demand Modeling. Cambridge, MA: Massachusetts Institute of Technology. Department of Civil and Environmental Engineering.

Federal Highway Administration. 1995. Office of Highway Policy Information. Highway Statistics Summary to 1995. Washington, D.C.

Federal Highway Administration. 1996. Office of Highway Policy Information. Highway Statistics 1996. Washington, D.C.

Federal Highway Administration. 1997. Office of Highway Policy Information. Highway Statistics 1997. Washington, D.C.

Federal Highway Administration. 1997. Our Nation's Travel: 1995 NPTS Early Results Report. Washington, D.C.

Federal Highway Administration. 1998. Office of Highway Policy Information. Highway Statistics 1998. Washington, D.C.

Federal Highway Administration. 1999. Office of Highway Policy Information. Highway Statistics 1999. Washington, D.C.

Federal Highway Administration. 2000. Office of Highway Policy Information. Highway Statistics 2000. Washington, D.C.

Federal Highway Administration. 2001. Office of Highway Policy Information. Highway Statistics 2001. Washington, D.C.

Greene, David. 1987. Long-Run Vehicle Travel Prediction from Demographic Trends. *Transportation Research Record 1135.*

Greene, David, Shih-Miao Chin, and Robert Gibson. 1995. Aggregate Vehicle Travel Forecasting Model. Oak Ridge National Laboratory. Oak Ridge, TN.

Hobbs, F. and N. Stoops. 2002. Demographic Trends in the 20th Century. U.S. Census Bureau. Washington, D.C.

Hu, Patricia S. and Jennifer Young. 1992. Summary of Travel Trends: 1990 Nationwide Personal Transportation Survey. FHWA-PL-92-027. Federal Highway Administration. Washington, D.C.

Hu, Patricia S. and Jennifer Young. 1993. 1990 NPTS Databook: Volumes I and II: Nationwide Personal Transportation Survey. FHWA-PL-94-010A. Federal Highway Administration. Washington, D.C.

Hu, Patricia S. and Jennifer Young. 1999. Summary of Travel Trends: 1995 Nationwide Personal Transportation Survey. Washington, D.C.

Klinger, Dieter and J. Richard Kuzmyak. 1986. Personal Travel in the United States, Volumes I and II: 1983-1984 Nationwide Personal Transportation Study. Federal Highway Administration. Washington, D.C.

Kuzmyak, J. Richard. 1981. Vehicle Occupancy: Report 6. 1977 NPTS. FHWA/PL/81/012. Federal Highway Administration. Washington, D.C.

Lave, Charles. 1991. Things Won't Get a Lot Worse: The Future of U.S. Traffic Congestion. Working Paper, No. 33, June 1991. Irvine, CA: The Institute of Transportation Studies and Department of Economics. University of California at Irvine. Berkeley, CA: The University of California Transportation Center. University of California at Berkley.

Martin, W. and N. McGuckin. 1998. Travel Estimation techniques for Urban Planning, NCHRP Report 365. Transportation Research Board. National Research Council. Washington D.C.: National Academy Press.

Newman, Peter W. and Jeffrey R. Kenworthy. 1989. Gasoline consumption and cities: a comparison of U.S. cities with a global survey, *Journal of the American Planning Association*, 55(1), pp. 24-37.

Oak Ridge National Laboratory. 2001. 1995 NPTS Databook. ORNL/TM-2001/248. Federal Highway Administration. Washington, D.C.

Pisarski, Alan E. 1992. Travel Behavior Issues in the 90's. Federal Highway Administration. Washington D.C.

Polzin, Steven E. and Xuehao Chu. 2003. Transit Market Share: A Look at New Data. *Urban Transportation Monitor.*

Real Estate Research Corporation (RERC). 1974. The Cost of Sprawl, Environment and Economic Costs of Alternative Residential Development Patterns at the Urban Fringe. Washington D.C.: U.S. Government Printing Office.

Schafer, A. and D. Victor. 1997. The Past and Future of Global Mobility. Scientific American. October 1997. pp56-59.

Schaper, Vincent and Philip Patterson. 1998. Factors that Affect VMT growth. Office of Transportation Technologies. U.S. Department of Energy. Washington, D.C.

Schrank, David and Tim Lomax. 2005. The 2005 Urban Mobility Report. Texas Transportation Institute. The Texas A&M University System. http://mobility.tamu.edu.

Sedor, Joanne and Harry Caldwell. 2002. The Freight Story: A National Perspective on Enhancing Freight Transportation. U.S. Department of Transportation. Federal Highway Administration. Washington, D.C.

Southworth, Frank. 1986. VMT Forecasting for National Highway Planning: A Review of Existing Approaches. Center for Transportation Analysis. Oak Ridge National Laboratory. Oak Ridge, TN.

Strate, Harry E. 1972. Automobile Occupancy: Report No. 1. Nationwide Personal Transportation Survey. Federal Highway Administration. Washington, D.C.

Transportation Research Board. 2003. Land Use and Site Design, Traveler Response to Transportation System Changes. Chapter 15, TCRP Report 95. Washington, D.C.

U.S. Census Bureau. 1995. Current Housing Reports. Supplement to the American Housing Survey for the United States in 1995. Series H151/95-1. Washington, D.C.: U.S. Government Printing Office.

U.S. Census Bureau. 1997. Current Housing Reports. American Housing Survey for the United States: 1997. Series H150/97. Washington, D.C.: U.S. Government Printing Office.

U.S. Census Bureau. 1999. Current Housing Reports. American Housing Survey for the United States: 1999. Series H150/99-RV. Washington, D.C.: U.S. Government Printing Office.

U.S. Census Bureau. 2002. Current Housing Reports. American Housing Survey for the United States: 2001. Series H150/01. Washington, D.C.: U.S. Government Printing Office.

U.S. Department of Energy. 1995. Office of Integrated Analysis and Forecasting. Aggregate Vehicle Mile Forecasting Model. Washington, D.C. http://www.ott.doe.gov/pdfs/vmtwhite.pdf.

U.S. Department of Energy. 2001. Office of Integrated Analysis and Forecasting. The Transportation Sector Model of the National Energy Modeling System. DOE/EIA-M070. Washington D.C. http://www.ott.doe.gov/pdfs/vmtwhite.pdf.

U.S. Department of Labor. 1993. Average Annual Expenditures and Characteristics of All Consumer Units. Consumer Expenditure Survey, 1984-1992. Bureau of Labor Statistics. Washington, D.C. http://www.bls.gov/cex/1992/standard/multiyr.pdf.

U.S. Department of Labor. 2002. Average Annual Expenditures and Characteristics of All Consumer Units. Consumer Expenditure Survey, 1993-2001. Bureau of Labor Statistics. Washington, D.C. http://www.bls.gov/cex/2001/standard/multiyr.pdf.

U.S. Department of Labor. 2003. Consumer Price Index. Bureau of Labor Statistics. Washington, D.C. ftp://ftp.bls.gov/pub/special.requests/cpi/cpiai.txt.

U.S. Department of Transportation. 2001. Summary Statistics on Demographic Characteristics. and Total Travel: 1969, 1977, 1983, 1990, and 1995 NPTS, and 2001 NHTS. Washington, D.C. http://nhts.ornl.gov/2001/html_files/trends_ver6.shtml.

U.S. Department of Transportation. 2002. Status of the Nation's Highways, Bridges, and Transit: Conditions and Performance. Washington D.C.

Wefa Inc. 2001. Vehicle Miles Traveled, for FHWA.